Words
by Eddie Izzard and David Quantick

Photography
in New York, San Francisco and London
by Steve Double

Virgin

Edited by Ian Gittins
Design by Leah Klein

First published in 1998 by Virgin Books
an imprint of Virgin Publishing Ltd
Thames Wharf Studios
Rainville Road
London W6 9HT

A catalogue record for this book is available
from the British Library.

ISBN 1 8522 7763 7

Printed and bound in Great Britain by Butler
and Tanner Ltd, Frome and London

To all the dreamers –
may their dreams come true

I'd like to thank Charlotte Knapton
for her love, support and help
with the book, and Jane Bussmann,
acid house queen of comedy.
DAVID QUANTICK

Thank you Tara, for being the light
that shines in my heart forever.
STEVE DOUBLE

Contents

Heroes, Villains
and *The Great Escape*

In the White Horse tavern, Greenwich Village, Eddie Izzard looks round the cool, tiled pub. 'Dylan Thomas was staying in the Hotel Chelsea, like I am,' he announces. 'He walked out, came in here and dropped dead. Just like I've done.'

Los Angeles. Backstage at a show, a promoter walks past, cigar in hand. 'Did I ever tell you what Mel Brooks said to me about Woody Allen?' he says to no-one in particular.

Steve McQueen was a hero. He was Action Transvestite. No, he wasn't, he was straight-on action. He never got into much transvestism. He did one big bearded film about a Russian philosopher, pre-revolutionary, someone like Dostoevsky. Some guy with a big old Russian name and with a big beard, who stood up for people against the Tsar, and he looked totally un-Steve McQueen. He could have played anyone he wanted, but he kept turning offers down. I think he got bored of these big roles.

There's a theory of not *acting* in films, just *being*, and in *Bullitt* he's almost *sub-being*, it's so sucked in. There's this guy he's supposed to babysit in a hotel, a guy that the Mafia might want to kill, he's a witness in a case, and the guy's saying to Steve McQueen, 'Look, you can't come in and tell me what to do.' And McQueen's just standing there looking at him and when the guy finishes talking, McQueen just goes, 'OK, um, stay away from the door.' He's ignored everything this guy said; he feels this guy is just scum. You realise he's been looking through him, not answering any of his questions. He says to his partner, 'I'll be back later.' It's this great thing; it implies such character status.

I loved that. And I loved him on the motorbike. I love *The Great Escape*, probably because it's British people getting it happening. So the boy trans-vestite adventurer in me is going, 'Yeah, *I* would have been there, *I* would have done that, *I* would have dug those holes...' It's actually a film about a whole bunch of thieves. It's a thieves movie, a heist movie almost, an 'everyone's illicit but it's all for a good cause' kind of thing. Everyone's trying to get out of that shithole and there's all the best of the worst: all the real bad escapers, someone who's escaped ten times, a guy who's escaped twenty times. The Germans want to keep an eye on them. So in the end they just put all the brains together: 'You're looking after this, you're the scrounger, you're the security guy.' I love it. It's got some hackneyed pieces: James Coburn's Australian accent does *not* happen. There's a character called Ives who goes 'Burds, man, burds' in a strong Scottish accent. He calls girls 'burds' and he says, 'I'm a jockey, I ride the gee-gees' and he's always in the cooler.

I will forgive certain things if I like a certain character. They can go through an indifferent movie and I will still like it

I've now realised that when Steve McQueen got away on the motorbike, he starts from Silesia, and Silesia is in Poland, and in fifteen minutes of screen time he went all the way to Switzerland... Jim Rockford, James Garner, has to get in an aeroplane and get to Switzerland, with whatshisname, Colin the forger, Donald Pleasance, who's losing his eyesight, and he nearly gets there. He's in an aeroplane and Steve's on a motorbike!

It's got a logical build-up to a logical crescendo, and I suppose it's kind of anti-climactic, but it's true as well. Seventy-six escaped and 73 were shot, so they did just murder them.

I don't know. I just love it. I will forgive certain things if I like a certain character. They can go through an indifferent movie and I will still like it. I can suspend my disbelief. But I was totally into *The Great Escape*.

Monty Python are big heroes. My dad was into it, which was good because a lot of parents said, 'What *is* this fucking stuff?' But my dad was into it, and my brother was into it, and *I* was into it. I went to all these

boarding schools where television was illegal; it was a sin from hell. I used to break into the TV room and watch TV at night. There was one television in this entire school and we used to leave the windows open and break in at night. I seem to remember watching the sitcom *Soap* in there...

I met Michael Palin in Brighton. I interviewed him first when I was at college, because he grew up in Sheffield where I studied. I thought, why don't I go down and interview him? and he said, 'Yes,' being kind of genial. Then when I met up with him in Brighton, I said, 'Do you remember the interview?' and he said, 'No.' Too many interviews, too many faces.

I met John Cleese. I asked him to come and see a show and he came. Terry Jones came too. Eric Idle came twice in Aspen. He's now buying one of the nights that I'm playing in Los Angeles. This is apparently a thing they do out there – they just buy all the tickets for a show. Which is kind of peculiar.

I still haven't seen all the television series, but the *Monty Python* records came in and I was learning all those like crazy. I really identified with Michael Palin. He could do all those disparate characters he was playing all these grounded caricatures and they were very different – 'Hi! Welcome to blackmail!' – and small crumpled guys and weirder guys, a whole range of characters. I used to repeat them; I thought I could do the intonations. Like the four Yorkshiremen – 'You were lucky, them days were bad, cup of tea without milk or sugar. Or tea.' I used to sit there in chemistry lessons and two people could do the routine; you used to share the parts out, batting it back and forth. I just thought, *I* could do this shit.

I would have liked to be in *Python* but I couldn't be in *Python*, but in the end I went on and did their TV special in Aspen which was so weird. They were doing this get-together, the first time in eighteen years, and I got this message – 'Do you want to be in *Python*?' 'Fucking hell!' Initially they wanted me to be someone who's just come along and go on the stage and they were going to say, 'Who the are you? Get off!' I was going to wear this ski hat and goggles, but then it was going to stand out too much. It would have been five Pythons and a weird invisible guy covered in heavy clothes. In the end I just came on wearing, you know, clothes...

There's a photograph of the Pythons which I keep on my dressing room mirror. They're all stood around laughing

Python broke America. *Ab Fab*'s done that since, and Dudley Moore, and Peter Sellers, but it's not a bucketload. And *Python* did it accidentally. John Cleese had been in a Footlights revue called *Cambridge Circus* over there in the sixties and they'd all gone around and got reviews from all the big-name reviewers. Or that's what it looked like. The big-name reviewers had names like Frank Rich or whatever and John Cleese and the others went out and found taxi drivers called Frank Rich and got them to write reviews.

There's a photograph of the Pythons which I keep on my dressing room mirror. They're all stood around laughing. just smiling and happy. Terry Gilliam's pulling a face, and three of them are fairly obviously playing waiters.

What they do is such a strange use of intelligence. They obviously know so much and they just talk complete bollocks... They would do things like summarise Proust in fifteen seconds, a joke I didn't get until Michael Palin explained it to me later.

I do the thing they do. They take large subjects and talk complete bollocks about them, and they take bollocks subjects and talk about them

in depth as though they're hugely important. It isn't topical but then that would date it immediately. *That Was The Week That Was*: do we watch lots of tapes of that today?

And they've been fantastically irreverent about Graham Chapman since he died. During the Aspen show, they brought his ashes on in an urn. And halfway through Terry Gilliam crossed his legs and knocked the urn over, so they all came and swept him up and said 'That's what he would have wanted!' They just kept taking the piss.

A gay man smoking a pipe.
Does that ring any bells in the lexicon of gay images?
There's some weird pipes, ones that go down to your knees.
They're small furnaces

Python did some vicious stuff. John Cleese and Graham Chapman wrote together and there was obviously a lot of bottled-up stuff between them. A lot of different bottling... You had John Cleese just trying to chill out from that austere sort of Englishness about himself, and then you had Graham Chapman being gay and not telling everyone and going round smoking a pipe, and it all came out in this huge rage.

A gay man smoking a pipe. Does that ring any bells in the lexicon of gay images? There's some weird pipes, ones that go down to your knees. They're small furnaces. They look good on native Americans. Two-handed fuckers.

So, yeah, *Python* were heroes.

As was Gandhi. Gandhi was pretty groovy and pretty thin. See, the trouble with Hitler was that ... he had a bad moustache. He said, 'OK, we'll get a million guys and we'll stand them in straight lines.' And the trouble with human beings is people just can't help looking at something like that and thinking, God, all this energy has gone into it, and then getting drawn in by it. Whereas I just think it's good that someone like Gandhi was marshalling all the energy in a much more positive way. And you can point out that person, Gandhi, to counterbalance the other person, Hitler, who seemed to get a long fucking way being a mad psychotic fucker.

There's that telling line in the Gandhi film where he says, 'A hundred thousand British people cannot run a country of five hundred million. We won't let you do it. Can you get out of our country, please?'

In the White Horse tavern, Greenwich Village, Eddie Izzard looks round the cool, tiled pub. 'Dylan Thomas was staying in the Hotel Chelsea, like I am,' he announces. 'He walked out, came in here and dropped dead. Just like I've done.'

David Puttnam was a big hero just because he was making British films happen. I wanted us to be playing on a world stage and I hated the idea of us *not* playing on a world stage. I wasn't there in the sixties when we were coming through and I hate the backwater-type idea. He was doing films that were going over to America, like *Chariots Of Fire*. And at the time one of my ambitions was to turn up on the set of *Local Hero*.

David Puttnam was really active and he ran Columbia, which didn't really work for him. He's moved into different areas now. He's more of an elder statesman. It was his global attitude I liked, not the fact that he seemed to be selling a pro-British thing. It's not the fact that people are saying 'We're British', it's the fact they're in Britain and saying,'Let's play on a world stage.' That's what I like. Like Alan Parker – he goes and plays the big fields and comes back with *The Commitments* and *Evita*.

I'm trying to make a film about Dick Turpin and Tom King, his partner who no-one really knows about. It seems Turpin was rather middle-class. He had private tuition and learnt Latin and shit. He was a butcher's son but he wanted the dirty life – the girls, the fast money, the excitement and

all that thing. He was quite a shithead. A downwardly mobile guy, but with a distinct ability as a self-publicist. He would do robberies and stuff that would make people write about him. He started developing what would end up as the dandy highwayman thing. He would say, 'This is a robbery, sir. I would like to have your watch and all your goods and money. Thank you very much. Now you may go, and tell people how well you were treated.' And they would go and say, 'Well, yeah! He was very polite, but he nicked all my stuff!' And the press would love it. This was someone revelling in it, like the Kray Twins.

I've been watching stuff about the Mafia, like John Gotti who would go round in all the suits. He was known as the Teflon Don because they couldn't get him on anything. He obviously thought he couldn't be touched... and then they touched him. There's another Don. This guy goes around in the streets of New York dressed in a bathrobe with a helper, just looking like he's nuts, but he seems to be the brains behind everything. He puts over this idea that he's insane so that if they do take him in, he's got this visual thing and people say, 'Oh, I saw him in his bathrobe – he must be nuts.'

Villains? Thatcher pissed me off. I really hated the eighties because of her. It was that 'I'm right and I know everyone else agrees with me' thing. Which is a thing I do, but in a comedy way. When I say, 'We all hate the national anthem,' I say the '*we*' in the Thatcher style – I imply everyone agrees with me even though I haven't asked them. She had that way of seriously condescending that just pissed me off.

And there was this whole thing of 'are they one of us?' That 'either you agree with me or you're fired' type of politics. I don't like it when people are that sure. It appealed to some people but a mature position is, 'Well, I'm not sure. This is *my* point of view and I can kind of see the other person's point of view.' But once you get to the stage of 'This is how it's going to be, and I know because I know I'm right' – the way she used the police to squash the miners' strike and bring in whatever laws to kill democracy, taking away the metropolitan councils and all that shit – I hate that.

And it seemed good that Thatcher was voted out by her own party in the end. She's still going but must be eating herself up. It must just kill her not to be in power. She'd obviously just lost it. And unfortunately that's what Hitler did. Hitler went, '*I do this, I am right*...' Now what is Thatcher doing? Pootering around. Training to be a plumber. She's been working for the Philip Morris Foundation, who are the people behind Marlboro. What's she doing? Educating people on how to smoke? Thatcher's there, fag in hand, going, 'Right... what we've got to do is get more of these cool but ultra-lite tar...'

There's that weird one about Edward VIII. Edward VIII was a Nazi sympathiser. Prince Edward made a documentary about him, and he was actually good at presenting. He seemed real and was quite engaging in defence of his grand-uncle. But I always say, 'That big handshake with Hitler, you can't really get round *that* one. You can't really be that pleased to see someone you don't like.'

I'm not excessively fond of the royal family. I think democratic monarchy could happen. If people want to keep the monarchy, they have to change this idea of 'ruling over the people' to 'serving the people'. Take the top 50 bluebloods and seed them like tennis, have play-offs or whatever, and have an election. Anyone who felt they had a right to the throne would go to the people and say, 'I should be king, I should be queen because of this or that. I'd put in *this* policy, I'd be a head of state. I would work hard to promote British culture abroad, the diversity of it...' They'd have to link in much more with human beings. The press would love it. It would be a huge public relations thing. It would pay off in all ways.

Although I'm OK with Charles. The Prince's Trust, he came up with that, for underprivileged kids. He's got a sense of humour. He's not hip,

Now what is Thatcher doing? Pootering around. Training to be a plumber. She's been working for the Philip Morris Foundation, who are the people behind Marlboro. What's she doing? Educating people on how to smoke?

but that doesn't really happen. I've always thought he was OK, that he had a heart, whereas his father seems to be from the planet Zog.

But Thatcher and Reagan... in America you stop being president but you don't stop being called 'President' and you go and open a library... I don't know what this library thing is about but they always do it. Ronald Reagan's library. I want to go down there. 'I want to get out the Narnia books.' 'The Narnia books?' 'They're all about this stuff in a weird world.' 'Did Ronald Reagan write them?' 'Well, he seemed to.' 'Can I order them?'

They've all got libraries, haven't they? All the presidents explode and they carry on being a president and I think they get a pension. And a set of teeth. Teeth for life.

There's a few things I like which I think are overlooked. Like *Robin and Marian*, the Dick Lester film, which is not seen very often and not hailed very often. It's a really sad film but I love that. Sean Connery and Audrey Hepburn. I'm a big fan of Sean Connery. Big fan. I love it that he's Scottish working-class and became a worldwide star. Like the way that the Hitchcock film *North by North West* is almost an English film, in that you've got James Mason (Yorkshire), Cary Grant (Bristol), and Hitchcock (Leytonstone). So a Londoner, a Bristol lad and a York-shire lad, big stars the lot of them, and everyone says, 'It's all American,' and it isn't and I like that.

Sean Connery is a star in a very cool position, who got out of the Bond thing, went into more difficult waters and came out through *The Untouchables* into a position where he can play something like *The Rock*. With great camera angles.

I did a Sean Connery impression to Sean Connery. Me and Julia Ormond who was in *First Knight*, were standing in front of him at the opening of *Art*. We were doing these Sean Connery impressions to Sean Connery and he said, 'Sho when are you going to do theshe impressions then?' 'I'm doing them now!'

If there's an actor who I aspire to be, it's Oliver Reed. I think of *Tommy*, *Three Musketeers*...that thing he had in *Tommy* I loved. In *Velvet Goldmine* I think I'm coming into an Oliver Reed area, which is a great place to be.

I really like Rowan Atkinson in the *Blackadder* Elizabethan thing. He's so sexy in that. And a bastard. He was such a shithead and it backs up my theory. Comedians can play shitheads.

I like Stanley Kubrick. I like Ridley Scott. I like Alan Parker. And I like Quentin Tarantino. Quentin Tarantino is right up my street. If I wrote a film I would like it to be like *Pulp Fiction*. I like the endless detail. Foot massage – 'Shall I give you a foot massage?' 'You know what that really means.' 'What does that mean?' 'Oh, you know what that means. Don't tell me you don't know what that means.' It's like, 'What do they call a quarterpounder in France?' 'They call it a Burger Royale.' Tarantino spends a lot of time on small things. *Pulp Fiction* is like *Coronation Street* with huge violence. Trivial everyday stuff like, 'Well, we've got to go and shoot this guy.' 'I can't now, I've got to go and pick my kid up... I'll meet you at half-five. We'll go there and waste these people then.' La, la, la. Everyday things. Violence, chit-chat and gossipy, weird stuff is blended in to make people freak out. And it *does* make people freak out.

The bit where they go over a bump and blow the kid's brains out works for me because they didn't fixate on the horror of the crime. 'I've just blown his head off.' 'I know, there's brain all over me...' I don't know where I would be in that film. On brain detail, probably.

I thought Tarantino's problem in that film was that he played a character too much like the character we know him as. He's got too much Tarantino baggage with him; he should be playing *vicars*. People *expect* him to say things like, 'I want to inject you with acid.' If he played straight people, there would be such an undercurrent. Like Richard O'Brien playing very straight people; there's an undercurrent of weirdness there. So, yeah. I link up with a lot of this.

I went to see *Get Carter* the other night. It's a good film. You could do it black or Hispanic or whatever. This thing of 'My brother's been killed, I've got to go back there...' One of those scenes at the beginning – 'We don't like you going back up there and stirring up trouble.' It's like *Hamlet* – apart from the fact it's very different.

Tarantino spends a lot of time on small things. *Pulp Fiction* is like *Coronation Street* with huge violence

I like Steve Coogan, Harry Enfield, *The Fast Show*, Mark Steele and Jeremy Hardy. Jeremy Hardy can attack things with a rapier, with a stiletto knife, and slice them apart in a very avuncular cardigan-wearing boy from Aldershot kind of way. He was being heckled at Jongleurs, and he did a light put-down on the guy. And the guy heckled again and Jeremy said, 'Oh… so you want to play, do you?'

I love the surrealism and the character stuff of Harry Enfield, like the Dutch policemen sitting in their cars. Harry keeps creating his characters and killing them. I loved *The Day Today*. That thing at the end where Chris Morris would turn and pull a wig off and long hair would flow out in silhouette. There are shows I've seen where I've thought, I wish I was in that show, and that's one of them, as is *The Fast Show* and Harry's thing.

Big stars are weird. Someone like Cher is very weird because in films she has this very classy, woman-in-control-of-her-life, kick-ass type roles, and in music… she came back and did that single with all the sailors on it. I mean – shit! It was so slutty it was unbelievable, stripping bare and sitting on a kind of huge navy cannon with all these butch sailors – butch sailors? *Camp* sailors. It was just so trashy. A bit like her music. I think of her in *Silkwood* where she played a fairly dowdy, normal character. Was she feeling, Oh God, you're saying I have to dress down and look like a woman who works in a nuclear power plant and lives in a trailer? Maybe she thinks trashy sells music.

Billy Connolly and Steve Martin are great. Steve Martin is brilliant at talking huge loud bollocks. I've got all these tapes of him – 'OK… we're innnn San Frannnciscooo…' He would sing these things and not pronounce them properly – 'San Francisconuh oh yeah oh yeah oh yeah – oh no…'

He would do nothing and say, 'Hey! We're having some fun now!' Just endless bullshit. It was all done in the big brash American voice, the one that Kermit the Frog has – sort of.

Billy Connolly is great just for his chat thing. 'Y'know when you see all these people who do these things…' One-sided chat, that's what it is. Two hours of chat and you don't get a word in edgeways.

Music really affects me and I love film music. The theme to *The Last Of The Mohicans*. It's just beautiful. It's by a guy called Trevor Jones and

Cher is very weird because in films she has this very classy, woman-in-control-of-her-life, kick-ass type roles, and in music… she did that single with all the sailors! It was so slutty!

his ten-year-old son's dyslexic, and he got into my stuff. He saw the shows and he started taking an interest in my dyslexically-minded stand-up. So I went down and did a talk at his school.

Basil Fawlty. *Rising Damp*. Rab C Nesbitt. You can have bastards in comedy. When comedies work they become classic comedy and when they don't work they become sitcoms. Rigsby you love to hate. The whole principle was wrong – him going into other people's flats. 'So, er, Phil, you, er, know about women?' I've never heard of a landlord who would hang out with his tenants. And the bizarre racism that runs through it, where you think, is this racism or is this being very satirical? And who knows?

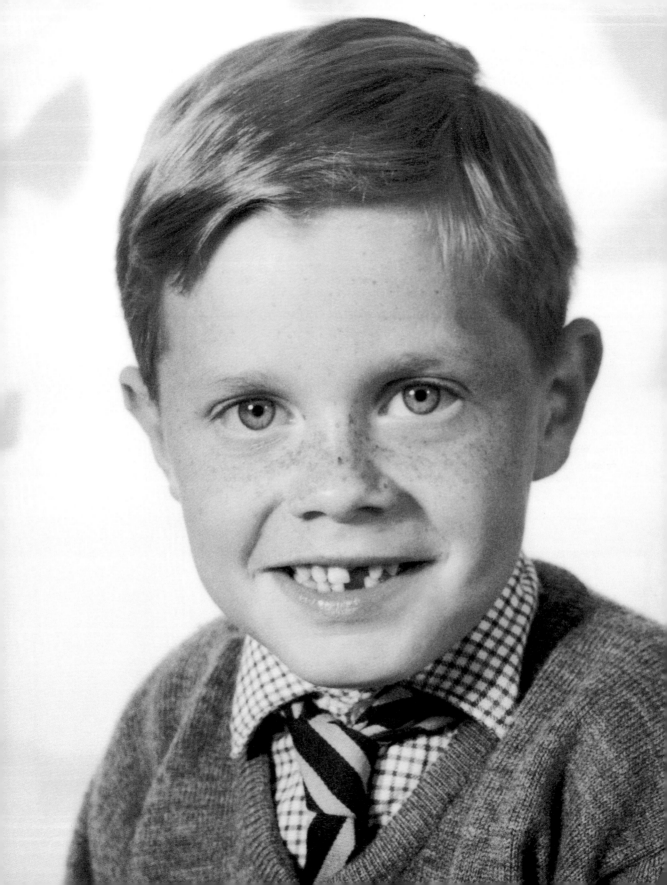

Julius Caesar:
my part in his downfall

New York: a lovely restaurant. Eddie Izzard is thinking about boarding school.

'I think I've wiped out some of the... more bad experiences from that time. I go back there and a lot of it's changed,' he says. 'They show me the new building but when you go away again you just remember the old school.'

Later he admits, 'I do go back to places a lot. I don't know why. Also I like looking back at the Izzard thing of being a Huguenot 500 years ago. I think it's a human need. It's like the American thing of being obsessed with lineage. I really like history, the fantastic stories that happen. I can't quite work out why, but I do go back a lot.'

I was born in February '62 in South Yemen. Dad was a fifties hippy with very short hair. He wrote essays on communism and stuff when he was sixteen. He joined BP as a filing clerk, not really knowing what he wanted to do. One of the first things he did was redesign the whole filing system so no-one knew where anything was except him, which I thought was a very good move.

He ended up taking this post in Aden, which is a bit like saying, 'I'm going to the moon.' It's still miles away, but this was in the fifties. Aden was a British colony at the time; BP had a refinery there and they built a town, roads and a hospital. My mother went out later when she'd decided she was going to be a nurse in Aden. So you had two people separately saying, 'I'm going to go to the fucking moon.' So then they met and got married and I was the second kid to come along.

I have an older brother. His name is Mark: he's a couple of years older than me. We've got a cinefilm of him running round playing football then poking me in the eye. There's a great little scene of him, me and my mother, he keeps poking me in the eye and my mother keeps pulling his hand away... And my dad's in other bits with the moustache he had at the time. Very 30-year-old.

With mother and brother

We left Aden in 1963. There was a revolution once we left... I've got to go back to Aden. My dad's going to take us and show us everything.

We went to Northern Ireland and we were there until '67 and that was great. BP had a refinery in Belfast and we used to go down there and hammer away on the electric typewriters. That was space age stuff to me. There must have been underlying political stuff happening but I was totally oblivious to it.

I was going to primary school and drinking these little third-pints of milk and the biscuits you'd get at break times and just drawing pictures of our house, Mum, Dad and stuff, and being in a gang and throwing mudballs at passing cars. Everything was being built then and they were constantly building bungalows, so we used to climb all over the roofs of them and pour water in all the cement mixers so it would all harden.

It was an immensely age-spread gang, from four to eleven or twelve. It was just the kids who lived on that street – Ashford Drive in Bangor. Some of them ended up joining the army. But it was a great time. And my mum was alive. I go back there and I remember it all. Asking for sixpence for ice-cream. Running like an idiot and then falling over and smashing my whole front tooth. There was blood and stuff and a lot of yelling but it was actually quite a neat tooth, with like a dunce's hat-shaped root coming out the top of it.

I kept it and gave it to my brother as a cufflink from a Plasticraft set, along with a toenail. This is how sick I could be. A bench had fallen on his foot, and a similar bench had hit my foot several months before, and so we had matching smashed toes. I don't know what happened to my toenail but his was preserved in this box so I thought, I'll put these two, my tooth and his toenail, in cufflinks and give them to him as Christmas presents. He was horrified. I couldn't work out why. I think he's still got them. They're these big chunky, Plasticraft, blue-based things, one with a toenail and one with a tooth.

I now think it's a work of Dadaist brilliance but my artistic career began and ended there with the horrified expression on my brother's face.

So, yeah. Northern Ireland. I left in '67 and moved to South Wales, near Swansea – a place called Skewen. That was very different to the essential green and rain and running around of Northern Ireland. I went back when I was 14. I said, 'I'm going to cycle from Sussex to Wales. I want to lose weight. I'll take no money and that way I won't eat and I'll lose weight.' But my dad gave me some money and a Little Chef map, which was the worst map to give me. I cycled from Little Chef to Little Chef, eating the maple syrup and ice-cream and orange fruities at petrol stations and going to farms and saying, 'Can I sleep in your field?' They'd say, 'Yeah. Here's a bit of water,' and I'd get woken up by cows who were just looking into the tent scaring the shit out of me.

When I cycled back the smells were so distinct they immediately hit me. The industrial smells of South Wales are incredibly strong. And there was that bit of the A48 as you go along from Cardiff along the M4 – it used to be motorway, motorway, motorway, then traffic lights. Traffic lights?! There's traffic lights on the motorway! It just changed to an A road for a stretch and then back to motorway.

But my mum died when I was there. March '68. So that was a killer, and rejigged everything. Before my mum died, they decided that me and my brother should go off to these boarding schools, because I think my dad had just got a career going. Having gone to Aden and whatever, he'd been promoted.

My gran (*right, middle*) used to work in a biscuit factory and cleaned houses and my grandad (*right, top*) drove buses, so that was a very working-class background. They were from north Bexhill, Sidley. I've gone back and done benefits there. No hot water, no bathroom, baths in front of the fire, an outside loo, that's what my dad grew up in. He decided me and my brother should go to boarding schools. A single-parent male, that's how you keep it all going.

So I was six when I went off to boarding school. There was a four-year-old kid there I felt so sorry for: he was still wetting the bed. I think that my child-like character that appears in my stand-up now was locked off at six. But my brother and I were both there, which was better than

With father and brother

just one of us. It was down in Porthcawl, a place called St John's School. It's like a desert island. There's beaches down there; it's very duney. I actually went back there and played a street performing gig as part of a Labour Party get-together outdoor something or other. Porthcawl had this funfair and a whole lot of stuff I didn't even know about. There's a Butlinsy feel to it which I found quite surprising because I didn't remember that when I was there.

I was a hustler. I would sell crayons in the school yard. 'You need these crayons. What if you get stranded on a desert island? How are you going to write a message? Crayons.' I'm actually quite fascinated in a very sad way by retail. I wanted to run a shop. You used to be able to get a little shop with those Hornby train sets and in the window it had all these things like Kellogg's cornflakes and tins of soup and stuff. You could look through the door and there was stuff happening inside... I wanted to sit in that shop. I like supermarkets. I just like hanging around the big aisles, and new things going up – 'What would I like today? Ooh, one of *those*...' It's a bit like *Spinal Tap* – 'Shoe shop...I could run one of those.'

We had a radio at school in Wales. I remember hearing Tom Jones' *Delilah* on it and *Those Were The Days* by Mary Hopkins, and it was a bit like hearing it from Mars. It was an old radio of my dad's from Aden I'd borrowed, so you'd tune in and you'd hear sounds from the outside. At the school you would sometimes get to go to this church on a Sunday, and when you're six it seemed like going miles, even though it's just down the road.

And there was this village playground with a door with a grating in it, which had scary steps going down to a well, where the devil lived, we all thought. You looked down into it and thought, where the fuck does *that* go? And there were these dunes and a caravan park which we'd walk through which would take us down to the sea, which was kind of cold and chilly, and there were lots of these yellow plants growing on the dunes which had caterpillars on them. We never saw anyone in the caravan site, because we were never there in the holiday season.

There was a locked-up centre at the caravan site, with arcade games in it. And there was a Dalek in there that you were supposed to get into and move around in. We had these horrible sandwiches and what they called lemonade which *wasn't* lemonade, it was some cheap stuff, and you'd have to bury your sandwiches in the sand because they were disgusting.

The food was awful, and I had a real food problem, a real basic palate. My brother was eating Indian food and I could only eat potatoes. That's why I wanted to be in the army because they were always peeling potatoes and I thought, well, I like potatoes, so… And this school served macaroni with warm milk. I mean, what the fuck was *that*? I've never seen that since.

And the best meal they had – they would take you down the swimming baths on a Thursday and you'd come back and have sausage and chips, and that was fantastic. There were some meals that you just looked forward to… they had compulsory tea drinking and I hated tea. But sausage and chips was the one meal I could eat.

We went on these school outings when I was at school in Eastbourne. I remember seeing *On Her Majesty's Secret Service*. I really rate the Australian Bond, George Lazenby. I love the film he's in; I am alone in that. But I challenge anyone to look back at it and say what is so bad about it. The fight sequences are great – they put these amazing sounds in, like they're fighting with planks of wood. These really heightened noises. Diana Rigg is fantastic, I like the skiing, I like Telly Savalas, I like the music… I knew 'We've Got All The Time In The World' could be a number one.

We used to get points, a school merit system, and they had sections. Everyone was in different groups and whichever group won the most points got an outing, and we'd win it year after year, and every year I didn't know what was going on. It was nothing to do with me, but every year I was just going on these outings, thinking, cool… but I haven't really helped with this. *On Her Majesty's Secret Service* was the film on one of these trips.

When I was seven I entered the sack race on sports day. My dad said, 'Put your feet in the corners and just run.' So I did and went steaming down the track. There's this picture of me going through the tape going, '*Yeahhh*,' fucking leagues ahead of the next guy… The next guy had just changed from his leaping style to a running style, because the sacks were too big and you could get a full stride in. I won a blue football. So that was me and my dad working together.

My dad's good. I think we're quite similar. We're a bit emotionally compressed; we don't get too elated by things because we've had bad stuff happen and more shit could be just around the corner. But we don't get too depressed either. We quite like pootling around but try to be more windswept and interesting, as Billy Connolly always said.

Now we work together sometimes in the community centre in Sidley the place where he grew up. My grandmother helped start it in about 1949. She taught me and my brother when we were at the kindergarten

> My dad's good. I think we're quite similar. We're a bit emotionally compressed; we don't get too elated by things because we've had bad stuff happen

Overleaf: shepherd, 6th from left

there. It's in Bexhill, East Sussex, where Spike Milligan was stationed during the war. He was on lookout on top of Galley Hill, waiting for the Germans to come. I sold ice creams at a kiosk at the bottom of the hill, and I used to cycle around looking for the places where he was stationed. The Delaware Pavilion, is where I sold sausage, egg and chips and cups of tea to old ladies: Spike played there, and I ended up playing there.

I did a stand-up gig in Sidley. I took a Hollywood searchlight, like the ones that used to sweep the sky for bombers. The last time these things were in Sidley was in 1942, wartime. We got permission – but the police were phoning up, going 'What the fuck's going on?' – and everyone was driving in from ten, twelve miles each way because they could see these lights in the sky. People kept driving up and saying 'What's happening? Can we come?'

It's nice working with my dad. He's treasurer at the community centre.

In 1969 we left Wales and went back to live in Bexhill. We went to school in Eastbourne – again, it was this boarding school thing. The first one was called St Bede's, right at the foot of the South Downs. The Downs has steep banks with loads of bomb craters because British planes coming back from missions would jettison their bombs on the Downs because they couldn't land with a bomb load, something like that, I don't know. We used to play in the craters.

I used to play a lot of football. At that time I *lived* for football. I just ran my arse off, playing left half and then right half. I was in the first team. I wasn't the best or the most gifted but I was good when the ball would go past our goalie and I'd be there to head it off the line. And when the guy was running ahead with the ball and he was bringing his foot back to kick it, I'd just put my foot in and knock it away from him. I'd do those things.

I couldn't kick the ball in the goal to save my life. I was scared of getting up there in case I tried and missed in an open-goal situation and then everyone would kill me. So I just used to do the good pass for someone else to knock it in. They used to read out the names of people in the first team in school assembly on match day – 'OK, get your kit and off you go' – and you'd stand up and walk out. It was great. I loved that.

But the second school in Eastbourne didn't fucking play football. What a crap decision. They played rugby, hockey and cricket and in the sixth form you were given an option of doing football. It was treated like pottery or martial arts. So I gave up on sport, really. I thought it was stupid not playing football. My brother had already gone to the school, so I knew about it. You accept it.

At university, I thought, hey, I'll get back into playing football, but I was so clearly five years out of practise. I was treated like shit by the people who played, because I couldn't kick a ball any more.

And it was no good with other sports. Cricket, the ball always tried to hit me. Hockey I liked but some guys could just look at that ball and *fbam!* – shoot it somewhere. I worked really hard to try and get good with the backs of hockey sticks and stuff but I couldn't hit it like the best guys.

I was in the football first XI at thirteen, though. Played 14, won 11, drew one, lost two. I almost played for my town. I was a reserve on the team. Eastbourne v. Seaford. I could have played.

My dad tells us that the 1966 World Cup was on television, and he was saying to us, 'You've got to watch, you've got to watch,' and me and my brother were saying, 'No.' 'You've got to watch, it's the World Cup –

St Bedes, 1970

it's 3-2 – it's 4-2...' And we were still saying, 'No' and sticking bits of Lego in our ears.

Supporting Crystal Palace is a bit of trial. What Crystal Palace do is go up to the Premier League and then go back down again. They have relegation battles. My dad goes to every home match and me and my brother go along too. We sit in the stand where my uncle used to sit. My aunt and uncle used to live across from the ground. We've sat there since 1969. I like Crystal Palace. Terry Venables is back again. Maybe our time will come. Somebody said to me, 'Is it too strong to say Crystal Palace are a joke team?' I said, 'That's too strong. You have to *die* for that.'

With stand-up comedy I'm probably doing some things where people think, how the fuck are you doing *that*? It's the same with football – how the fuck do players put it in the goal like that? When they do these penalty shoot-outs, I look at them and think, *I* couldn't place it with that power.

I wanted to be a professional footballer. I didn't think I was going to make it, because I didn't seem to be that good, but I really loved it. I know people don't equate football with transvestism but the fact is, there's *got* to be a lot of football players and football fans and people in the army, navy, airforce or driving forklift trucks who are TVs, because it's male tomboy. It's

kind of like male lesbians because we all fancy women as well. But if you embrace it, you get certain gifts from the feminine side.

I tried to get into plays at school but I couldn't because they were convinced I was crap. Maybe I *was*. I would audition but never get a role.

I learned the clarinet for the wrong reasons. I was trying to play the piano but I ended up playing this clarinet and I had to be in the school band. They put on a musical, *Oliver!* or something, and I had to play the bloody clarinet. One kid at school's dad was a semi-pro actor, so he played Fagin and he had his own make-up and his own stuff and my big treat was I would hand him his hat and his cane. It was my big 'My God, I'm almost in the play' thing.

So from the age of seven I really wanted to act and I did really weird things to try to get into it. I did *Joseph and His Amazing Technicolor Dreamcoat*. The choir at the school was doing it, and I wasn't in the choir, so I just hung around them and lifted things and pushed things. And eventually I was in it, and I even managed to get a solo line out of it.

We did a version of *Beauty and the Beast* when I was seven and I was a street urchin. The street urchins combined had one line – 'Oh Beauty, don't go' – which, when the line came up, I used to say really quickly before everyone: 'OhBeautyDon'tGo.' All the other kids would go, 'Oh... he's said it.' So I would make it my own line. Upstaging... Because the chorus at seven was a bunch of dopey kids. 'There's a star...' 'Wha...?' 'There's a star...' 'Wha...?' 'You're a shepherd.' 'Am I? Oh yeah...'

There was a flu epidemic when I was seven so I was not only in *Beauty and the Beast*, I was a shepherd as well. So I was in two plays. I was a featured shepherd. After that the parts were very lean. I couldn't get into any of the big musicals – *Pirates of Penzance*, or any of that stuff.

They did *Julius Caesar* and I played Trebonius. Of all the conspirators against Caesar, Trebonius is the most boring. One, because his name sounds like trombone and two, because there's a line where they go:

OMNES   See, Trebonius knows his mark, for look how he leads Mark Antony away so
         that Mark Antony will not be there when it all gets really tough with Caesar
         and we stick all the plastic daggers in with the syringe of blood attached.
         So that means Trebonius won't have a plastic dagger and a syringe of blood
         because he'll be standing in the fucking wings when it happens.

I wasn't on stage. I'm just in the wings with Mark Antony going, 'Ah, they're doing it with the old plastic daggers.' There's ten conspirators and nine of them are on stage stabbing Julius Caesar and there's one in the wings, going:

TREBONIUS   I'm not fucking *there*.

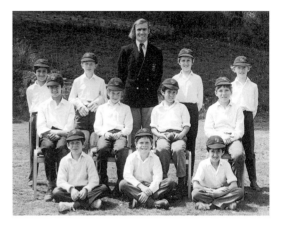

Rugby: left, front row
seated on grass

Cricket: middle, front row
seated on grass

Football: fourth from left,
middle row

They used to take photographs in dress rehearsals and there's all these conspirators with their plastic daggers, except for one kid who's got the syringe of blood facing the camera. One kid called Caldwell, who was…*shot*.

I did get into one thing, though. I always liked comedy, and when I was twelve I got my first laughs. We did this revue in a class taken by a teacher called Sam Grey. He was kind of different. Apparently he got married and he had this motorbike trip around South America planned so he went and did that instead of a honeymoon. Watergate was happening at the time and he used to read the tapes out to us. He told us how to say 'breast' in French.

And Sam Grey did this revue, and we were doing all these sketches we'd written and I got distinct laughs on a solo bit. It was a mime thing. This guy was bowling to me and I was supposed to be a cricketer and I was batting the ball away with supreme confidence and arrogance, looking for the ball in the distance then realising I'd smashed the wicket. I remember thinking, hey, I've got laughs here!

And then I discovered Peter Sellers. My dad had his records and I remember trying to do the accents. Trying to do an Indian accent before I thought, this actually gets me into a difficult area, because if you do different ethnic accents from around the world it can look like you're taking the piss. I do a routine about the Welsh guys carving Stonehenge and I try to make sure I'm not taking the piss. There's these rather effete druids and the Welsh guys are going, "You fucken basstards!"

So I was at St Bede's and…yeah. I was very fit then. I did a lot of running about. The sea is at the bottom of the school and the Downs are at the side. We used to get up at seven o'clock in the morning and walk through the sea to the reef. It would cut our feet to shreds.

Photograph caption on blackboard:

1ST XI
Results for 1974
Played 14
Won 11 Drew 1 Lost 2

You'd hear large booms in the middle of the night, where an old World War Two mine had hit the cliffs. The school chef was a coastguard and he used to have to go out and make sure there were no others. When I was there, a searchlight would pass across the bedroom window every night from Sovereign Lighthouse. I used to go to sleep with *wshhh* – this flash of light going past the window. Which you got used to.

We had the coal strike as well, which was great. Lessons would end and there was no food, so we had to eat crisps. We were making tents and putting candles under the bedclothes.

I like things that *work*, even in difficult circumstances. I like doing gigs, even when I'm fucking dying. I'm trying to do a website and I want it to be real cutting edge. I like *pushing* things like that. We do merchandising on the tour and I want to make the T-shirts so they last. Quality.

So, St Bede's. It was a good place. The head teacher there was a decent guy but he had a strong thing about not putting me in plays. I went back and harangued him recently: 'You didn't let me be in any plays.' 'Oh, I'm

sorry.' 'But you didn't let me be in any plays!' 'I didn't know...' 'Why not?!'

I have a big love of the South Downs now. They're kind of bonkers. On the north side they don't have cliffs, they just slope off like a big-steep-forward-roll-possible-all-the-way-down type of hill.

At thirteen, I went to Eastbourne College, but I had to take the first Saturday off because my dad remarried (*left*), which I thought was fun. I missed French. 'Sorry I missed French last week, my parents got married.'

In my first year I was taught about the slide rule. They said 'The slide rule is important. Without it you can do nothing. The slide rule is the modern weapon of efficiency. With the slide rule you can get from here to the stars. Buy it, use it – your slide rule!' Within one year it was, 'Burn the slide rule. The calculator can add up with none of this fucking sliding the shit around and working out where that bit in the middle goes. Smash it over your head.'

I had a nice plastic slide rule and everything slid up and down and you would put this bit *there* and move that bit *up* and – ah! Approximately 1400. Sometimes it couldn't do it, and it would just approximate things. I saw a film where they were all going round in spacecraft and they were doing it all with slide rules. 'How far to Pluto?' 'Approximately 1400, sir.'

At my first Eastbourne school a fifth of the pupils were girls. Maybe a quarter. At this school, there were no girls for three years, and then there *were* girls. So it was just…odd. At sixteen there were girls again but only one girl to every ten boys, so packs of spotty boys would follow these girls around and carry their… everything. Literally put them on a litter and carry them around. So I didn't talk to girls for a whole year. I thought, '*I'm* not going to be able to pull. I can't say I'm in the first team.' Only by the end of the year I had started using my wit. I could say, 'Yes! I am from outer-space!' Or some such shit.

I believe in co-education all the way, although boys benefit more. Boys tend to say to girls, 'You're not *working*, are you?' and put them off.

At my last boarding school, they had compulsory cadet things. This was all marching about, running about on hilltops, hiding from people and going 'Bang!' It seemed like a great game of Cowboys and Indians, if not terribly real.

I was brought up on these books about the war. I know war is hell, but I sort of wanted to be involved in that struggle. It was something to do with not taking in the reality of it all, but the derring-do. Derring-do? That sounds really crap – but the running jumping climbing standing still part of it, *that* was the reason I wanted to be in the army. The reality is that apart from the Second World War, most wars are politically messy. The Second World War was straightforward, 'These guys are bastards and they're trying to invade everywhere. Let's stop 'em and let's defend our country.' So I link up on that patriotism.

I went on a special course, where I was kind of disillusioned, because I didn't do very well. I was in this group and we weren't winning things, until we did orienteering, which I was great at from the Scouts. There's a whole logic of map-reading: you take a bearing and then you've got to follow that bearing even if you think you're going wrong. Because even though the compass is pointing in one direction, you tend to think, *this* isn't the right fucking way, but then you're just lost. So with orienteering we did all right.

We did an ambush exercise. We were all in the back of this army truck going along. There were three trucks, and they stopped. One guy who had done this kind of thing before, said, 'It's an ambush! Run for it!' So everyone leapt out of the trucks and started haring out into the undergrowth. And then some sort of colonel type came by and said, 'Look, you're not supposed to run away at this point. Could you come back, please? And you're captured.' 'No, we're away! We're back in Blighty.' 'No, you're not. You're all caught. And you have to go to the concentration camp.'

We got taken to a 'concentration' camp. Concentration camp's a big word for it. It was like a walled, barbed-wired, enclosed area, and we were all supposed to crouch down on our haunches, so it gets really achy on your legs, with your hands behind your head. And then we worked out, 'We're supposed to escape from here,' so after a while somehow some of us got out. And then these soldiers would chase you, shooting blanks at you, and you had to try and hit them with bits of wood. It was all very basic.

There was this paratrooper guy there and I tried to talk to him. I said, 'So what's it like being in the army?' and he said, 'Fuck off.' So I thought, well…I appreciate you bringing me on and encouraging me.

There was this other kid who had been on this cadet course. He got promoted and I didn't. I just thought, *this* is kind of arbitrary, isn't it? I knew that I'd done just as well as him. Because I thought the idea was if you showed willing and went on this course, you'd get more stripes and all this kind of stuff.

In fact, I'd bought a set of colonel's pips. So I used to walk around with colonel's pips on and a handgun I'd bought in France – it was like a starting pistol. We went on exercise on the Downs and they said, 'There's going to be an ambush today, you're going to be ambushed' – which is great, so we went out with .303 Enfield rifles, waiting to be ambushed. And before we went, I was doing all this action with the rifle, loading it and unloading it and stuff, until I broke it.

**Clarinet: third
from right**

**Drummer: centre,
front foreground**

I had broken my gun, so I had a large rifle that didn't work, and this pistol, and my colonel's pips. So I got there and we were all just wandering around, waiting for the ambush – and then, 'Ambush!' And so everyone gets down on the ground and we're shooting away, they're ambushing us and we're ambushing them. We've all got things that go bang, basically. We're going 'Bang bang'. And they're going 'Bang bang bang', and we're going 'Bang bang bang bang'.

After a while, we start thinking, we're not getting hit doing this, so we start standing up and going 'Bang bang bang', Obviously this would make us die in real life – but we realised we weren't actually killing anyone, so we started shooting at anyone. I just went around with my pistol, shooting at my own people. Bang, bang, bang – a crazy afternoon.

They said, 'All right, you've done very well in that, except you're all dead and you all cheated. Now you've got to get back into Eastbourne without getting caught by, I don't know, Nazi stormtroopers or something. So do it by the cunningest method you know.' Everyone was going around the Downs, so me and this guy called Paul Wedge went down to a bus stop and got on a bus, when the schools were emptying out at about four o'clock. So we took a bus into town with a load of schoolkids as our way

of getting back. Which I thought was the initiative thing; the SAS thing.

We were sitting there with rifles and uniforms, surrounded by kids all staring at us. We made our way back and got in early.

It was a weird time. I was driving parallel ideas. There was no way you could be a comedy performer in the army. The ENSA thing didn't really happen. I was talking to Billy Bragg about it. Billy Bragg's the only person who's been on *Top of the Pops* who can drive a tank.

The SAS was advanced running, jumping and standing still. Blue berets and very secretive. They were all self-sufficient so if one member of a platoon got killed, then the others knew what to do. It wasn't like, 'Oh, he was the explosives guy. We're going to have to do explosives without him.' 'I don't know about explosives. They go bang, don't they?'

But it wasn't making any sense to me because I just wanted to do comedy. There was just an idea that performing comedy was crazy, but as I got closer and closer to sixteen, I just thought, this *is* possible. I wasn't running around anymore, so I wasn't fit, and I didn't get promoted so I thought, bugger that.

And after the course, I obviously thought, if merit isn't rewarded then, fuck it, I'll go and be a transvestite.

Animals and Comedy

New York. Eddie Izzard is being interviewed by MTV. He tells the perky journalist, 'You get extra points because you're British. Because you're European, in fact. People go, "Oh you must live in a castle." If you play in Britain first and go to America, in Britain they're quite pleased. If you do well in America first and then you go to Britain, they're…not.'

'Eddie, that's great,' says the perky journalist. 'If you could infiltrate my questions into your answers that would be fantastic.'

Eddie looks a little puzzled. 'If I could infiltrate your questions into my answers…you want me to repeat your question at the beginning?'

The perky journalist beams. 'I don't want you to be set in stone,' she says.

I used to be – not a household name, but a garden shed name. Trowel. I thought I was a trowel. You'd go, 'Trowel? Oh, trowel, that's a small thing…' then I felt I was up the garden path, and now I feel I'm in the door. I'm not like 'pint of milk' or 'hoover', but I'm like 'hatstand' now.

And that's fine. I'm very wary of things escalating. It's good that I can sit in cafes and restaurants without a lot of hassle going on. One person might come up and say something very nice and complimentary. I don't know what to say when that happens, because you can't go, 'Yes, I *am* fantastic, thank you. I agree with you.' You can't do that, and it's quite an effort to block it all. So the easiest thing to do is say 'Thanks' and carry on and just forget about it and keep buying bags of crisps.

There's this whole thing of stand-up. With rock'n'roll, people become gods on stage; they become very sexy. Film stardom is also sexy and godlike. Comedy is about speed of mind, observations; it's what's going on in the head and how you can physicalise that. You're the audience's representative on stage. You're the bloke who went up and said, 'Here, I got an idea! You seen these things? I know a few things.' It's just someone who gets up there. And if you get successful, you stop being that ordinary person and you become this special guy who gets swept in on a sedan chair or whatever.

There is this bit of material I still like – I was laughing at it myself – which is that sometimes you go to the loo and there's no toilet roll. And

you've just got to get out of there and buy a toilet roll. But you can't just go to the shop and get a toilet roll because they'll look at you and go, 'Big poo now.' And you don't want *that*, so you buy a Mars bar as well. You go up and say, 'Mars bar – oh, and a toilet roll as well.' And they're looking at you with that face of, 'Big poo now. Mars bar's a cover. It's a front. You don't even want a Mars bar. It's big poo now, isn't it?' You're implying, 'No no no, Mars bar. Big poo maybe never. I'm buying the toilet roll for a friend. It's a present.'

I went to get a toilet roll the other day and I immediately went and got something else with it, even having said this material in my head. It's really odd when you start acting out your own material. Hopefully that's because it's true.

You've got to be careful as a comedian, if you're successful. You've always got to be able to buy a packet of crisps. *This* was the point I was trying to get to. You've got to be able to say, 'I was in the supermarket getting these crisps and this guy came up to me' and 'What's this weird thing they're selling now?' rather than, 'I sent my butler out for some crisps and he said this funny thing.' And then the audience is going, 'You're not going to be one of *those*, are you?' You've separated yourself, and there's a distance between the average person and the person on stage, as opposed to in the clubs where you really *do* feel like one of them.

I want to be able to talk about reality. I think you've got to try and keep it on a real scale. Because if you say, 'I was going on Concorde, I got out

I could easily get into the tabloids if I shot someone, or killed someone's gran, or invaded Russia. Those are obvious ones not to do

of the limo, you know like you do, and Boutros Boutros Ghali was there, and I said, Boutros!' – you'll just get lost up the end of Boutros Boutros Ghali.

If you were *extremely* famous, you could say, 'I went on the tube the other day, like I used to do in the old days, and no-one recognised me. I was really pissed off.' And you could talk about the whole ego problem.

Maybe I'm talking less about shops nowadays. I got more into history, which I thought was wide open as a stand-up subject.

So I'm *quite* famous. This tabloid area seems dangerous. Like this recent story about me being the new Doctor Who. It was totally made up, but I could see where they're coming from journalistically. The story was 'Doctor Who – should it be a man or a woman? There's a new film coming up... what about Eddie Izzard? He's kind of weird bonkers.' It just becomes a good story. But I'm not really tabloid, which I'm pleased about. I think that's a fantastically double-edged sword, when they're all writing stories like: 'Eddie Izzard yesterday went to a shop and bought a sock.'

Some people seem to do things that make the tabloids head straight for them, like get in fights. They like certain things. They like the bad boy thing – you do a bunch of bad boy stuff and you'll get in there – or shagging – who's shagging who or who's breaking up with who. I'm at the stage where I could easily get into the tabloids if I shot someone, or killed someone's gran, or invaded Russia. Those are obvious ones not to do. I don't think I'm quite in that bracket. I go to things and there's paparazzi and they go, 'Eddie, Eddie! Over here, Eddie,' and they take all these photos, and then the photo editors go, 'Well, *no*.'

Then you go to America and it's on a different level and they're going, 'So you are an average Joe who's just got up there.' 'Well, I'm an average Joe who wears a ton of make-up.' Your average transvestite.

They have some extra weird ideas in America about Europeans. They think we're all really classy and we all live in castles, which we don't. It's like we think Americans are all rich and live in a big house in some mountain, or that they're all film stars or have oil wells. So I assume I must carry some of that European baggage and then the transvestite thing must just move it into a weird area where maybe they link it back to seventies David Bowie. I don't know.

They know how to celebrate you, but they also know how to cut you dead when you go away. Whenever I leave America, even if I've been away for less than two weeks, it's a bit like I'm dead. It's like if you're not there generating a buzz, your calls drop off. They're very, 'You're here, you're doing it, you're great… no, you're gone, you're dead.'

I'm trying to sidle across into other areas from comedy. Once you get a profile in one area, you can get work in other areas and it doesn't seem to matter where you come from. I suppose it depends – if you were Benny Hill or Jim Davidson doing a film like *The Secret Agent*, there would still be press on it. They would say, that's a spin on it, but they're roles that would not necessarily get well received. I didn't realise that when you get well known in a certain area, you get called up and asked to open supermarkets. Although I haven't actually been asked to open supermarkets. God, the times I've been *desperate* to open supermarkets…

Comedians do get asked to be whatshisname in *A Midsummer Night's Dream*, the guy with the pig on his head, or the guy with yellow things in *Twelfth Night*, Malvolio ... but fuck those! I just said 'No comedy roles.' I said to my agent, 'Look, I want to get into straight roles, I want to get into a young Oliver Reed area.' Just because I'm kind of *bigger* rather than thin and reedy. It's that distinct power that I liked. I like playing shitheads. There's an affinity between the extreme of comedy and extreme of shitheads.

If you imagine someone like Jerry Seinfeld playing a real evil fucker you can really get into it, because you think maybe that's what they're like – jolly on stage but bastards in real life. There's a fun in it. But believing in someone like that being a romantic hero – no. If you are in comedy, playing shitheads can be a way in to straight roles. Roy Hudd in *Lipstick On Your Collar*. Leonard Rossiter used to play shitheads before he got known. If you do enough serious roles, like Robbie Coltrane did, you'll cross over.

My idea for staying off telly was purely so I wouldn't get too locked into comedy. Then I realised I can do a *few* things like chat shows and that doesn't cause a problem because I can just sit there and talk crap, and then make a point or say whatever I want. It doesn't get me so locked into this thing of being 'The Comedy Person'.

People who've crossed over: Woody Harrelson, who went from *Cheers!* to *Natural Born Killers*. Richard Briers, who has a scene in Kenneth Branagh's *Frankenstein* with Robert De Niro. It's *The Good Life* meets *Taxi Driver*. 'You talking to my dahlias? I don't see any other dahlias around...'

I've found you can't sing *The Good Life* theme tune. We sat around when I was doing *Edward II* and we couldn't. It goes: ba ba buh ba ba buh, ba ba buh – bub bubububh. It doesn't pass the old grey whistle test.

Career-wise, going away and coming back works. Errol Flynn had a second career where he played washed-up drunks. Joanna Lumley in *Absolutely Fabulous* was great as a drunken, crazy witch-fiend. She played it with such relish. Like that could actually be her after *The New Avengers* – a crazy drinkin' woman. People like it when someone comes back and plays the dark side. Michael Caine came back in *Mona Lisa*... He could have returned after *Mona Lisa* and played a number of those roles, but I don't think he really wanted to.

But I'm up for doing chat shows to promote things and films for telly.

I'd like to do a *Simpsons* or *Wallace And Gromit* type animation where I could do the voices.

I did *Have I Got News For You?* and they asked me a question, and I said 'Jam' and it got a laugh. The next week the Daily Mirror editor, Piers Morgan said 'Jam' on there because I said 'Jam' and it didn't work at all. He said, 'Well, you all laughed when Eddie Izzard said it,' and Ian Hislop said, 'Yes, but Eddie Izzard's *funny*.' If you're a comedian, you can engineer a position where you can say weird crap and get away with it, but there's no way you can come in and just *copy* the weird crap.

I like doing *Have I Got News For You?* but it's quite difficult because to do it properly, like Paul Merton, you have to read all the newspapers, and you'd have to go through tons of them, which isn't my thing. Also, actually sitting in the seat is quite tricky because they make you lean back and whenever the camera cuts to you, you're just sort of slumped, going 'Wuhhhh'... I just started doing what Paul was doing in the end. He'd just stare off into the distance and then say, 'Brown jacket.'

Doing stuff like that on telly is a fairly good place to be as long as you don't say 'Jam' too much. 'He just goes on and on about jam.' Which I do quite a bit. Jam is a comedy word. Jam is one of my first jokes. It was the first really stupid one. I used to start the show at the Comedy Store and your opening joke had to be the best one. I used to come on and say, 'Went down the pub and had a few jars. Went to another pub and had a few jars. Then it was someone's birthday and I went back to their place and had a few jars... After that I thought, phew! That's enough jam for me!'

It's a joke that only works in Britain, but it did have the power to kill.

Richard Briers has a scene in Kenneth Branagh's *Frankenstein* with Robert De Niro. It's *The Good Life* meets *Taxi Driver*. 'You talking to my dahlias? I don't see any other dahlias around...'

Occasionally I come up with punchlines. There was one on my video that all the journalists wrote about, which was 'Bees make honey. It's so weird, because... do earwigs make chutney? Do spiders make gravy?'

There are a lot of animals in what I do, although I've been trying to phase that out a little bit, even though Pants Cat is a character I want to keep going.

I had some sort of line where a pair of pants were lying about and I said a cat would steal them and wear them on his head because he was Pants Cat. 'Pants Cat! Pants Cat!' and I just went into this stupid thing, a bit like Captain Transvestite or Captain Non Sequitur. I liked Captain Non Sequitur: 'Help us, Captain Non Sequitur, there's a boy trapped down this well.' 'Look. I've got a cheese sandwich here.' 'But Captain Non Sequitur, the well is going to explode in two minutes.' 'Do you like my new jeans?' 'Well, yes, but...' He just says anything that's not connected.

Captain Transvestite would turn up with a lipstick at any point. 'Look down the well.' 'Here's a lipstick for you. It's called Crimson Delight. Goodbye!' 'What can we do with this, ya stupid...transvestite?'

So, animals. Yeah. It's a Gary Larson type thing. You get the animals talking in the way Calvin and Hobbes use it and Charlie Brown used it, you get creatures to talk in a very coherent manner. Then I think you see human beings in an objective way. You go, 'Bad dog!' and the dog goes, 'Why am I bad dog? Define bad.' 'You stole a biscuit.' 'Well, so what? There are crimes way worse than stealing biscuits.' 'Well, yes...'

> You go, 'Bad dog!' and the dog goes, 'Why am I a bad dog? Define bad.' 'You stole a biscuit.' 'Well, so what? There are crimes way worse than stealing biscuits.' 'Well, yes...'

Pants Cat has now developed into this great cartoon. There's Sock Dog as well, who's wearing a sock on his head, and there's worms going, 'Cool, Daddio,' and wearing sunglasses. Very beat generation. And there's a gerbil living in a cage. It's all in a house and the animals have their own social level and interact just like humans.

Pants Cat's always there, and the gerbil's going, 'Got to get out of here man. I want my lawyer, talk to my lawyer, got to dig my way out, man. It's hell in here,' like he's in prison. It gets so much reaction. People have written to the *NME*, 'from Pants Cat in Glastonbury'. It took off quite quickly. It's sitting there waiting to happen and I can't work out whether to do it as a *Simpsons* or a *Wallace and Gromit* Claymation, or do it as a book like Gary Larson.

I did the cats drilling for oil routine. It came up accidentally. I was talking about cats purring and I said, 'They're not purring, they're drilling for oil.' I did a spiel about a cat looking round the corner of a sofa

Pet Cemetary,
Presidio, San Francisco

and everyone thought, oh yes, that looks like a cat. Then I had the cat saying, 'No, I'm not drilling for oil – that's purring mate.' But then the cat goes back behind the sofa, puts the goggles and big gloves back on, drills some more…

And then the cat theme came back with *The Great Escape*. 'I had three cats wearing trousers down the bottom of the garden, digging a tunnel.' I had another thought about cats and dogs' 'thumbs' being halfway up the legs, and I said that genetically or evolutionarily wise, they're moving. But are these 'thumbs' moving down to join their hand or going up to end up on their head? If they go down, they're going to end up with a grabbing paw, an opposable thumb, and then they're going to pick up a gun and say, 'I want my fucking cat food *now*…'

Superstitions are linked to cats. If a black cat crosses your path, it's bad luck. In some areas, it's good luck. So… what does *that* mean? And when is it crossing your path? If it turns to cross your path can you cross its path before it crosses your path? Can you jump over it? Superstitions have got to get their science together.

Walking under a ladder – I always walk under ladders. I cross black cats. I shout Macbeth on stage. I will be performing and sometimes I say, 'Macbeth. It's very bad to say Macbeth onstage because Macbeth is one of the Macbeth bad things to Macbeth say on the Macbeth stage…' I go on like that. And you're not supposed to whistle in the theatre, because all the people putting up the scenery were all ex-sailors who used to deal in whistled commands at sea. So it's bad luck to whistle on stage because they drop a picture of Castle Elsinore on you.

I'm still not quite sure why I do animals. But it's like Gary Larson. He had cockroaches hanging out in human situations and you get this wry look at human behaviour.

Like the routine I do about the dog who wasn't happy with his wash… which all got confused. There was a dog getting a stick and there was a callback to some previous line in my act about, 'Are you happy with your wash?' and the dog was running to get sticks and going back to his master and saying '*There's* your stick. What, you're not going to hold on to it? Why can't you hold on to the stick? I mean, just… keep hold of it! I can't keep going and getting it for you!'

If the routine is in some way believable, the audience buys into it. If it's not, they won't go with it. You say, 'Ants rule Mars' and they'll go, 'Hmm, I don't know…', unless you have a good reason *why*. But Neil Armstrong getting it wrong and going, 'I'm a small man for a giant and… oops, sorry Houston,' – well, everyone can get the idea of that.

Can't they?

Male Tomboys
and Action Transvestites

New York: the foyer of the venue Eddie Izzard is playing is plastered with enlarged photocopies of reviews. 'QUE SARONG SARONG' says one. Another reads, 'WHY HIS SILLY BRIT WIT IS A HIT'.

On stage Eddie reveals why his first performance in Paris was not a success. He tells an enthralled audience, 'They weren't up for it, and the French for transvestite is "*travestie*".'

Later he muses, 'I hate that idea of, "It can't be done." "I want to be a transvestite and go to America." "Oh, it can't be done."

Probably I am the only transvestite comedian in the world at the moment, in the non-Lily Savage sense of the word. There's the transsexual woman who won the *Eurovision Song Contest*. Is that the same? She's better looking. 'She's gorgeous, so that's fine.' If I was gorgeous, that would be different. Julian Clary's gorgeous. I'm this... *bloke*.

People say, 'Why don't you change your clothes at half-time?' Why? Do footballers do this? I'm not a drag act. This is not about the clothes, it's about the comedy and I just do whatever I want. I can wear whatever I want now. When I first came out, a comic called John Gordillo did a video of my first gig in a dress, and in the video he's talking to comedian Jo Brand and he's saying, 'What do you think the reaction's going to be to Eddie being in a dress?' She said, 'The same reaction as to me wearing a dress.'

I don't think there are many *out* transvestites in the public eye – transvestites in the sense of male tomboys. I've been looking to find them. There's a lot of gay and lesbian people who are out and there's men who use drag *per se*, dressing up as women, and then there's rock stars who'll put on eyeliner and could well be TV – but I don't think they are. I don't know where Mr David Bowie stands at this time.

I worked out I'd better come out and I just did it. I actually came out when I was 23 (1985) and then I sat in a cafe and told the *Observer* I was a transvestite halfway through 1991. I wasn't wearing make-up or anything. And then people started saying, 'Well, I've never seen him in a dress,' so I thought I'd better go on to the next stage. I wasn't actually

 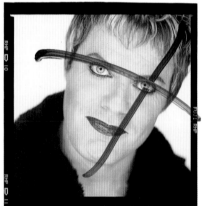 

meaning that I should wear skirts on stage or whatever, but then I thought I should do that if I wanted to. I should have the freedom.

When I first came out, I went to see a bank manager, a dentist and a doctor, wearing a dress. I remember going to see a dentist wearing make-up. He was looking at me with all the make-up on and I was saying, 'I've got a bad tooth.'

I went to see the doctor wearing make-up:

'I've got a cough.'

'You've got what?'

'I've got a cough.'

'You're a transvestite?'

'No, I've got a cough. I *am* a transvestite, but I've got a cough.'

'Well, I'd better sort the transvestite thing out. Have to refer you for that.'

'No, that's not a problem. Just the cough, thanks.'

I dared myself to go to all these places because I thought if I did it, my confidence would grow. So I did. It was scary, but scary is interesting if it's positive. Once you've done it, you realise it's not as scary as you thought it would be, therefore your scary receptors change. 'Fear is the mind killer': one of the great lines in *Dune*. I love *Dune*.

I took a train back to Sheffield, where I was a student, and I had a friend there I thought might kill me for being TV but he just turned up at the station and picked me up on his motorbike. Lucky I wasn't wearing a skirt.

Then there was the fight which I had in the street in Cambridge. It was after the third gig of my tour – Cambridge Corn Exchange. Sold out, got a good review on *The Late Review* – they gave me a clean sweep of yeses,

Germaine Greer and everyone, and I get the impression they tear the shit out of things, normally. I was sitting on my bed going, 'Hey, this is really good.' That was my second show. Then the next night I did the third show, went out afterwards and had a fight with these guys.

I don't think I was enormously transvestite that night. I wasn't wearing the skirt and the fantastic Versace boots, I was just wearing the trousers and heels and make-up, and this black jacket I wore in New York – my lucky jacket, that. It's now got a hole in it. So this guy stopped and said to his mate, 'Look, it's a transvestite.' He went, 'Ooh Tracy, ooh Tracy, ooh Tracy.' So I did all my streetlore-type stuff:

'Look, you live on the street – have respect. You don't need to do all this. We're just two individuals on the street – have respect.'

'Ooh Tracy, ooh Tracy.'

I've gone very big on the Tracy line. We've now got tour jackets with My Name Is Not Tracy written on them. It has to be said in a Michael Caine voice.

So he was going, 'Ooh Tracy, ooh Tracy,' and I was going, 'Look, seriously, have respect. Why do you need to do this?' And he hit the 'Ooh Tracy' line a third time – magic three – and I said, 'You're a cunt who deserves to be cut with a knife' – which I repeated in court – and then he went for me. I was doing quite well, I was blocking away. And then four other guys were suddenly there. And I thought it was just me and him, but of course the way to win a battle is superior numbers.

So they were all beating away and my friends were trying to pull them off me. I was doing well with this bloke, I got about four hits in. And at the end I was still vertical. It was probably over in 30 seconds. Then they sauntered off and went into this pub disco about 50 yards away. So we were all staring at each other and they were talking to their bouncer friend – who turned up later as a witness for them. He told the court, 'Yeah, he attacked five men at once,' then he went and sat down and joked with them at the back of the court.

The police turned up and said, 'Was it squaddies? Was it squaddies?' 'Squaddies? Two Oxford dons, mate.' They kept saying, 'Was it squaddies?' like it was, 'Oh, we have tons of squaddie fights. They're constantly beating up transvestites round here.'

Anyway, two of my friends went into the disco to point them out, and there was a kind of hyperactive bouncer there. They couldn't find the troublemaker. I went in there and I couldn't see these guys and this bouncer asked me, 'Is this him?' And this guy, who *was* one of them but who was the pacifist, appeared and he was saying, 'Look, we didn't want any trouble.' I thought, Oh, if *you're* here, the other guy must be here. And I looked round and there he was, dancing in the crowd, Happy Mondays-kind of dancing.

So I picked them out. And in the police van on the way back, he apparently said, 'Yeah, I did it,' and he admitted everything. The police never told me that. I felt more bashed up than I looked. We had to give the police all the details and for some reason I had to show them the physical evidence so they could note it down. The bruises.

And then three months later, when I'd forgotten everything about everything, I had to hire a car and go to court. And everybody was going, 'I've forgotten what everyone looks like. It was just some guy you saw for two minutes three months ago.' You can't remember what you said in your statement because it was three months ago. They said, 'Can you identify

We've now got tour jackets with My Name Is Not Tracy written on them. It has to be said in a Michael Caine voice

the man in court? Are you sure it was this man?'

They put the witnesses and the defendants about 50 yards apart. It wasn't a great situation. Intimidation is common, especially in the toilets, which you share. It would be very logical to put the witnesses on one side and the defendants on the other so they don't meet. Think about what intimidation serious villains could do.

Anyway. We couldn't remember what the bloke looked like, but he was stood there, going, 'Ello darlin'! Argh!' being the chirpy lad he was, and we went, 'Oh, it's him! That's the guy.' He'd identified himself when we couldn't remember him. He decided not to talk in court. And we'd all seen *Crown Court* on TV, so everyone was there ready to do their thing:

ME	It was him, m'lud.
MAGISTRATE	It's not m'lud.
ME	All right.
MAGISTRATE	And only answer when you're spoken to.
ME	All right.
MAGISTRATE	And don't point out anyone in the court.
ME	Oh, right. Can I say what he looked like?
MAGISTRATE	Yes.
ME	Well, he looked like him.

So we went up and said our thing. I was there in a sober suit with make-up saying, 'Yes' – it was 'Sir' and 'Ma'am', they couldn't get enough of it – 'You're a cunt and you deserve to be cut with a knife... I was very angry.' They were very understanding. And then the defence witnesses went up and they couldn't deal with being in court, and the usher had to say, 'Stop laughing! Stand up straight.'

And since these guys had worked out that I was this so-called notable person, they weren't saying, 'And then this bastard over here...', they were saying 'Eddie' – 'Matthew hit Eddie and Eddie hit Matthew.' And then they were saying that I started it. I came out with this line which I now use in the stand-up – the idea that no magistrate will believe you put on make-up and then go out looking for a fight: 'Do you want some? Do you want some?'

It was very important to wear make-up for the court case or their imaginations would have run riot. 'What did he look like?' 'Oh, he was up to here with the stockings and the wig on.' The image of transvestites is so negative. It's like American television; I have to do every interview in make-up to tell them, 'This is what it's going to look like, guys. This is going to be the Marc Bolan end of transvestism.'

I went to Downing Street in make-up. I was pleased New Labour had won, I've been a supporter. I was invited to go along and the tabloid newspapers said, 'HE WILL WEAR A TUTU!' I was supposed to be one of the most dangerous people who could turn up. Me and Noel Gallagher. I thought, if I just go wearing a sober suit and some make-up and some heels, they'll be fine – everyone's going to go, 'It's fine! He's not wearing a tutu!' The tabloids opened the gates for me by saying I was going to be really extreme.

I've learnt that you've got to be really non-apologetic. Never apologise for being TV. You've got to say, 'Hi, I'm here, can I have a cup of tea? And one of those biscuits?' If you say that, it's fine. If you go in and say, 'Excuse me, I'm a transvestite, I'll be in the corner, I won't be a problem, I'll face away,' everyone will go, 'Oh–oh, problem case in the corner.' So don't apologise. I picked this up from Madonna.

I notice that people say, 'Well, fair play to you. It's your life.' I said this to my dad when I came out: 'I think the British public will be able to deal with it if I say, this is it, I'm OK with it, just chill out.' This one guy in Cambridge obviously wasn't so sorted out with that, but that's OK because I've had big hulking guys come up and say positive things. I think it's positive if I stick up for myself. That's how you can register with football fans.

If I had my life all over again, I'd be a transvestite again. Even though it'd obviously be much easier *not* to be. A lot of TV's don't come out because then you're just a bloke who fancies women. But there's this whole female side in your head that's a big secret and such a burden and when you come out, it's 'ARGHHH! Got to tell everyone!' But once you're out, when people say, 'Are you a transvestite?' and you go, 'Yeah...' and then there's nothing else for them to say.

Stealing lipstick at fifteen was the first public manifestation. It was a vastly public manifestation because it was a meeting with the police. My mum died when I was six. I was apparently interested in her stocking tops, according to my dad. I knew I was TV when I was four. I saw somebody wearing a dress and I thought, *I'd* like that. It's genetic, it's in the chromosomes. It's in there and it hasn't changed at all.

I've thought about changing sex but I look too much like a bloke to change sex, and I actually appreciate the male side more by being able to express the female.

People say, 'Why aren't you wearing make-up?' and I say, 'Because I don't *have* to.' Make-up is fun, but it's laborious. I can't always be bothered. It's the lazy bloke thing. I'm still very slobby. Women have a better sense of smell. That's why men smell terrible – and women tell them about it.

Transvestism is *not* drag. I've being trying to avoid this pigeonhole. I seem to have been allowed a certain amount of freedom because what I do is just keep moving around. If you wear make-up all the time, then people expect you to continue to wear it all the time. If you wear no

If I had my life all over again, I'd be a transvestite again. Even though it'd obviously be much easier *not* to be

make-up half the time, then they say, 'OK, you're going to go both ways then.'

On the *Glorious* tour, when I was on stage I didn't wear any lipstick but I wore more eyeliner. It's like Keith Richards – he always shoves on eyeliner for gigs and interviews. In fact, I don't think I've ever seen him without it. And it's because it works for anyone, male or female. It makes the eyes just... *kick out* at you and it's definitely for boys in rock'n'roll. But it has to be badly applied. When I'm trying to get fucked eyeliner, I have to tell the make up artist that *I'll* do it, because they can't do it. They are trained to do a very smooth line, and it's like learning to drive well and then someone saying, 'Drive badly.' It's quite hard to drive like when you were a learner. You have to really work at it to do it so badly.

Usually, if I want to look more fucked, I just sort of shove the eyeliner on to make it look ... more fucked. The truth is, I've got kind of bored with make-up now I have access to it. Like women do. You'll see a lot of women around in their twenties and thirties with a bit of mascara on and that's all they bothered to do.

Drag can feel like trying to be a woman and I don't think that I can quite do that. I think in the end it's down to the way you look. Julian Clary just puts on make-up up like I do, but his image is very different from mine. He would put on make-up and just look more female than me. It's your bone structure. It all happens at puberty – male coding and genetics kick in, and it broadens the jaw and all this shit.

From being into the SAS to coming out as a TV was kind of an odd traverse round, but I know there must be a lot of people in the armed forces who are TV. You've got this large streak of bloke in you, which is why a lot of TVs drive forklift trucks or lorries or are in the Forces, but you've got this feminine side trying to get out. A lot of women say I'm very male about things. It's kind of 'male lesbian'. Butch lesbian but a male version. It's confusing. I haven't worked it all out...there's obviously a number of lesbian women in the armed forces.

I go for the straight line theory of sexuality. Everyone is somewhere on the straight line. Sex is encoded into the foetus after a couple of months and sometimes it's encoded in an unusual way. We're all human units. We have this male and female thing, but society wants this big fucking motorway between the two sexes. We're all somewhere along the straight line and we're all a mix. And if you admit the mix...people seem to respect what you are.

I was always looking for something to stand for. Playing France happened because I decided, 'I *want* that.' I want to go to places that people say, 'I wouldn't go there,' about. That's also part of me being a TV: people say, 'I wouldn't do that.' Then you go, 'Well, *I'm* doing it.' It's kind of edgy and exciting and stupid. But in the long run people go, 'Oh, of course!' My whole gigging in Europe idea is, once you've done it, people go, 'Oh, maybe *I'll* do that.'

Coming out as a TV, I felt that I could go out and ask six billion people, 'Should I come out as a transvestite, seeing as my stand-up career's starting?' and they would all go, 'No – no – no – no – no.' Everyone would say no. And I thought, It's the right thing to do. And then other people said, 'Oh, you only got your career going because of the transvestite thing.' You can't win. Being a transvestite is *such* a boon to your CV...

I was on *Question Time* and we were talking after the broadcast about how tall people are. David Dimbleby said, 'Well, I'm five foot eleven and a half but I tell everyone I'm six foot.' And then he said, 'I don't know why I'm telling you but you make me want to be honest.' And I thought, that's not *me*, it's because if you're there with someone who's said they're a transvestite and they're sitting there with a bunch of make-up on, there's no point exaggerating half-an-inch of your height.

I find a strength in trying to be open about things. But then some people think they really know you and they try to sit in your cab with you and things. Which is a bit much. But I met Jerry Sadowitz recently and he said to me, 'You make people go away happy,' which made me feel good. Especially seeing as I went on after him at the Comedy Store and died on my arse in 1988.

I find my dreams have changed. My dreams are pretty good now. There's one recurring nightmare I used to have when I was a kid. I would go into a small room with a table and an overhead light and there was a – person of restricted growth – on the other side of the table, who chased me round and round. That obviously meant that I was going to be very very good at maths.

The first nightmare that I had in Northern Ireland was one where I was being chased by Indians. I must have been about three or four. Now, I think Indians are noble warrior people with a fascinating religion, but then they were scary characters on the television to me.

But the interesting thing is, from then on, I started fighting back in my nightmares. I actually give my nightmares a bit of fucking aggro now. I remember one typical nightmare where I'm buying a baked potato. 'Baked potato.' 'Here's a fiver.' 'Oh, we're out of baked potatoes.' But he won't give me the fiver back. 'Can I get my fiver?' 'No. No change.' 'I gave you a fiver.'

'No you didn't.' Suddenly he starts attacking me. So I cut his head off with an axe. It seems really extreme, but at least I fight back.

When I was younger I felt the world was on top of me. But as you fight the world and the world sometimes gives in, you think, ah…maybe you've just got to fight a bit on these things. I think it's linked into the fight-in-the-street type thing.

I'm proud that my nightmares only give me so much hassle. I fight back.

Those tripping over in bed dreams are quite funny. Just lying there and – *wuhhh* – and you're all horizontal and you think, how did I fall over? And they all mean something oblique, don't they? It means you… like cherries.

If ever I decided I was going to wear a dress in a dream, I'd always wake up just before I got the opportunity. Until I came out and then it sort of relaxed. It was such a fucked-up area in my head. Before I'd be asleep and then suddenly it would be, '*Zzzah*! O-kay! Good morning! It's four a.m.! Time to wake up!'

I always thought it would be quite good fun to play a girl in one of the school plays, but I never played a girl, and this was in my cute days when I could have passed for a girl more. I was seventeen, at college, when they said, 'Right, you're playing the girl,' in this revue we were doing. I said, 'Oh, wow!' and then psychosomatically I got ill the day before the show. My brain couldn't deal with it. I got flu, or a cold or something, I was quite incapacitated. It was just not being able to deal with this situation.

I remember when I was 21 this one friend of mine saying – chit chat, chat chat – 'Have you ever worn women's clothes?' And I remember my mind going, that's the one question that's right at the heart of the problem, and my voice going, 'Ahh… ggh…ay… hyuh…uhh.. no. No! NO!' 'Oh.' It's going all the way in and alarm bells are going off – AWOOP AWOOP! Dive dive dive. All right, man the decks! Batten down the hatches!'. I had to lie down in a dark room to think about being TV and how to get on top the situation.

Your brain helps you with things you don't understand. That's how people block out car crashes and horrible events – the brain can help you by shutting down when you get to a difficult area. So when I got to this area, my brain wouldn't let me concentrate on the idea. I had to sit there. I was trying to think, *why*? *Why* do I feel there's this boy/girl fight going on inside? *Why*? 'Why' seemed to be very important. I still haven't got an answer. I just pulled the curtains and lay in a room and tried to go through it – real self-analysis.

I tried to go to a psychiatrist when I was at college but they didn't get an appointment for me. This is true. They just couldn't get it together. I

went down to the student health centre and they refer you and send an invite through to where you're staying. But it didn't come. Then I met this doctor, who I'd unburdened my big secret on to, in the street. I said, 'My appointment hasn't come,' and he said, 'Oh, hasn't it? I'll get on to it right away.' But still nothing. If I was him, I would have made sure. I'd have checked to make sure the kid was OK. Potential suicide.

I *wasn't* actually a potential suicide. I knew that, but he didn't. Maybe he was a casual, playing-the-odds type doctor: '50/50 he won't commit suicide. I can't be bothered to follow it through.'

So I gave up and in the end it was all self-analysis.

It was hard to come out. I was living at Highbury Corner, and I found a TV/TS hotline. I thought, ah! I plucked up enough courage to call them and they were in Upper Street, just down from where I was, and just round the corner from the police station, which was a very bizarre thing. There's a block of flats there now. So I went there. I was very fashion-restricted then. I was wearing God knows what – combat trousers and Jesus sandals, a complete visual mess. I used to wear whatever was there, whether they went together or not.

They were very helpful. I manned the transvestite helplines at some points. We could wear whatever we wanted there. Certain people would

turn up with their wives and people would change there. It was good, but it was scary being open. After a while I got to know a few people. There was a transsexual there who I thought was a woman. There was a lesbian woman who visited there too. I first went outside with her as a TV – we met up in Regent's Park, I think. I went round with ridiculously high heels and my feet hurt like crazy.

It was kind of strange and underground, manning the helplines. People were phoning up like they were sexlines – this was before sexlines – and asking 'What are you wearing *now*?' The person, Yvonne Sinclair, who ran the place said, 'If you get one of these sexline calls, say, "Sorry, the line's gone fuzzy," and ring off. Just pull the phone out of the socket."' 'What are you wearing?' 'I'm wearing a hat and a balaclava.'

I met this lawyer guy who said, 'I can't take it that far because I'm a lawyer and I can't be out.' He said being transvestite was a gift. I thought, *that's* a good line. He said it plain and simple: 'This is a gift'. Obviously, it didn't feel like a gift; it felt like a curse, initially. I now feel it opens up an amazing way of talking to women that you don't get as a Mr Deep-Voice-Type-Man: 'Oh, I'm a man, a very male man, going out to cut some wood.' I can just say to a woman, *'That's* a great lipstick.'

There's that OJ Simpson thing that colour becomes insignificant when you get to a certain level of fame, and it's similar with sexuality. Back in the Danny La Rue time, they'd say, 'Oh, he just does it for fun. He's really a rugby player.' 'He comes from the tradition of pantomime, men dressed as girls and girls dressed as boys, and it's all just fun and it's all just nothing to do with anything.' *Now hold on...*

They've done studies and found that there is a gay gene thing. I think that means there's a lesbian gene and a TV gene. It would be good to prove it, but there's a downside: 'I don't want my baby to be gay, I don't want my baby to be lesbian, I want to terminate this pregnancy because it's a gay baby.' In fact, you get such fabulously talented people who are of alternative sexualities because of the mixture. This is my whole thing about the mixture of races and cultures, which I think has happened all down the ages. This thing of the Aryan pure idea is doomed to genetic subnormality and the *mixture* of the genes promotes strength.

Mongrels are always brighter than pedigrees. My stepmother's into poodles – which I used to call Russian hunting dogs when I was younger, which apparently they were. 'Russian hunting dogs! Fierce!' When I was growing up, these two dogs were just crazy bonkers dogs. One was the

They've done studies and found that there is a gay gene. I think that means there's a lesbian gene and a TV gene. It would be good to prove it

Clint Eastwood of dogs who would run around. He'd chase you round the sofa and then you'd stop running and he'd keep going.

That was an early bit of stand-up for me, which no-one laughed at. I'd say, 'God, it's so much fun! My dog…' He'd sometimes get outside the house and you'd try to get him back in and you had to tempt him with chocolate sweets and you'd put one down and he'd come up to it and you were going to grab him when he got it but he knew you were going to grab him, so he'd snatch it and run off.

He was also a cat. He behaved like a cat. He would do cat washing-face stuff.

The word 'poodle' conveys this image of effeteness, and there's all this thing of carving shapes out of the dog's hair. I mean, they are actually made of wool. But they were originally hunting dogs. I used to say that only three things have haircuts: sheep, humans and poodles.

But I saw the breeding chart of those dogs and it was all like, the grandmother mated with the nephew. All inbred out. And there's that

Hair on mammals is a very strange thing. Why is it dotted in certain areas? And why do beards grow *here* and not *there*? What are the patterns of hair? I mean, who worked this out?

other breed, the one with all the folds of skin on its face. Bulldogs? Pugs? They've got more skin than face. Now what is the point of that?

Hair on mammals is a very strange thing. Why is it dotted in certain areas? And why do beards grow *here* and not *there*? What are the patterns of hair? I mean, who worked this out?

And then there's this thing that women grow hair on their legs and shave their legs. Or *some* women do. There's this whole thing with gender. There's a number of mannish-looking women and a number of feminine-looking men. Julian Clary's a beautiful man but he's not a transvestite. If he was, people would think he was a woman but that's not his bag. And that would not happen to me. No matter how hard I try. When I first came out people kept going, 'Yes sir, yes sir,' so I gave up on that.

Alternative sexualities and orthodox sexualities: that covers it for me. You try and keep away from the word 'normal' – normal and normality and normalcy as they say in America – but certain people do go, 'Oh, I just like dressing up. It's nothing to do with sexuality.' Hello! This *is* sexuality!

Upstaging
as a Career

New York. The woman from MTV persists. 'Does being English make you funny?' she wants to know. Infiltrating her question into his answer, Eddie says, 'No. I don't think being English makes you funny. Otherwise there would be about 40 million people over here making a living.'

London. 'When I told my Dad what I wanted to do, he just said, "As long as you're happy." For about five minutes I said I wanted to be an architect. Then my dad said, "You can't draw!"

'I remember there was a guy in Birmingham signing on in those years when you could still decide what work you wanted to do. He didn't want to work, so he said, "I want to be a shepherd." In Birmingham. He didn't get much work.'

Literature always baffled me at school. Shakespeare intimidated me: 'What does it *mean*?' I thought it had to mean something exact. I couldn't work it out. But I could add up. Maths and chemistry. I got a B in those. Physics, D. I think physics is probably more interesting when you're not pressurised to learn it. All that space and time and Stephen Hawking and Einstein – that seems interesting physics. But the way it was taught at school, it bored the brains out of me.

I got the A-levels so I could go to Sheffield University and do accounting and financial management with mathematics, a dual degree that just seemed very long and impressive. I was trying to get to Cambridge just to do the Footlights. I saw the Griff Rhys-Jones and Clive Anderson and Jimmy Mulville year of the Footlights on telly and I thought, Oh, *that* must be the way. Then I found out that *Python* had been in the Footlights but then I couldn't get there because I wasn't working hard enough.

My first problem was the fact that I couldn't get any acting roles. And then I thought, Well, I can't do romantic lead roles – 'Dahling, your eyes are full of...' but I could say, 'Dahling, your eyes are full of furniture. They make my ears explode with delight.' I could say rubbish versions of it. I could do comedy.

I got into Peter Sellers, and *Python* and early Benny Hill. I used to *hoot* at that. The whole family used to watch that. We used to record it off the telly. We'd put the tape recorder in front of the television and tape it. I taped the *Goodies* and early Benny Hill. Later on, just more and more naked women came in, chasing balding men. He was under all this pressure to churn out all these shows.

I learned how to steal scenes, as an actor. My first stealing thing was when I was at school. After the first Eastbourne school, where the teacher wouldn't give me any parts, I went to the second school, where I auditioned for things but nothing really happened. The fourth form did a play every year, so I thought, *I* could be in that play. But then the year I got into the fourth form, they stopped doing plays. I mean, were the breaks happening or not? Not – it seemed.

Then I auditioned for *A Comedy of Errors*. After I auditioned, the teacher sat me down – because it's always teachers who put these things on – and said, 'What part are you looking for in this play?' I thought, what a question. I said, 'You know those really big parts, when you're on stage all the time and you get the girl and you have all those lines and you're heroic? Something in that area. That sort of big, leading part.' And he said, 'How do you feel about the jailer?' And you think, it's the fucking jailer again. Yeah, all right...'

But the jailer is handcuffed to the leading actor in *A Comedy of Errors*. The director, this teacher called Andy Boxer, who gave me the best breaks at school, had seen Trevor Nunn's production with Richard Griffiths as the jailer. Richard Griffiths did this thing where one of the two twins separated at birth is handcuffed to the jailer, but handcuffed through a chair.

So you've got the lead character and the jailer handcuffed together through a chair. Big comic device because you're going round with a bloody chair hanging between you. And in our version, the lead guy was quite tall and I was quite short – I was fifteen. So he kept spinning round and I

I got into Peter Sellers, and *Python* and early Benny Hill. I used to *hoot* at that

would be spun round the stage, hanging on for dear life, so I played that up.

I wore this Cromwellian helmet with a visor that went up and down. It had this bobble in the top, like a circular loop of metal, and another teacher said, 'You could thread some string through there and pull the visor up and down.' I got four strands of black cotton, tied them on, threaded them through and round the back. I did a dress rehearsal where I had a tankard of beer in some sort of tavern, and I was there with this visor coming down over my nose, trying to drink. I kept my hand behind my back like a policeman on duty and when I pulled the cord the visor lifted up. It killed the audience. People were saying, 'It's not really Shakespeare, is it?' 'Fuck, I don't care, it got a big laugh.' Actors were going round to watch it. The teacher let me keep it in, and it brought the house down every night.

After that I got given two other parts. So I realised that stealing scenes leads to better roles.

We had a deal at college: whoever upstaged the most had the scene. So it was 'Upstage if you want, but *I'll* be upstaging *you*.' We had certain scenes which were kind of boring, like we'd have a lot of chat in one

scene and then we'd have a scene that was almost entirely plot. 'So then what did they do?' 'So then Roderick phoned and then the person came and brought the bag of soot to Mr Greengager.' And my partner Rob Ballard was in the background, eating fake grapes off a plastic grapevine, and throwing them up in the air. Just to upstage everybody. He won.

You've got to be wary of upstaging in professional terms. Like in *The Avengers*, I can't upstage Sean Connery. You've just got to upstage in the most casual way. Move the eyes a bit more to the left.

I played the Nazi in *Cabaret*. I had red hair – the colour my beard goes. I slicked it back, thinking, this'll look more Nazi, but it didn't look right, so I dyed it jet black. Red hair slicked back just doesn't look Nazi. I was up for an *Eastbourne Gazette* Local Oscar for being 'Superb as a Nazi thug in the making'. That was my first bastard part.

In my teenage years, I definitely wanted to do comedy and get into something like *Python* on telly. I went to Sheffield, and I thought, 'Stuff all the work. I've done enough work now. I'll just do shows.'

I went show crazy because I just wanted to get into comedy. There was this guy, Steve Daldry, who was at Sheffield at the same time as me, who did *An Inspector Calls* and ran the Royal Court. He was doing a version of Bram Stoker's *Dracula* at Sheffield. Another guy was doing Howard Brenton's *Workers of Happiness* which was billed as a 'comedy.' My lack of knowledge of literature and books is phenomenal, so I auditioned for that for the comedy angle... whereas Bram Stoker's *Dracula* was done in a quite camp big way and I should have been in that. Then I did an American comedy thriller called *The Gazebo*, which we totally rewrote and ripped apart. We rolled a turnip across the stage all the time... 30p a ticket. It was terrible.

I also did a revue and took it to Edinburgh. It had a dreadful name – *Fringe Flung Lunch* – and was on at twelve noon in the Celtic Lodge on Lawnmarket, opposite Brodie Tavern. Eighty-seater, bad time, bad show.

There was a gymnastic sketch where people came on – 'We are from Bavaria.' Or 'Rumanian jumping bats.' And two of us would go on and shout 'Hey!' and just lean over a bit. Instead of doing fantastic things, you'd just lift one leg off the ground – 'Hey!' Big noise. The sort of thing everyone would think of in the school revue.

One day we just got hysterical because there were about three people in the audience and no-one was laughing except us. I remember saying to the other guys, 'Oh, let's just get off.'

We had a pilgrim sketch. The Wife of Bath and all these people turned up at the inn and the guy said, 'No room at the inn.' The nativity got into it somehow. 'There's no room at the inn.' 'No, no, we are the pilgrims.' 'No, there's no room at the inn. It's a stable.' I think that's a better idea than the one we had. 'There's no room at the inn. Herod is taking a census.' 'No, no, we're pilgrims. This is England.' 'No, this is Nazareth...'

And we had one guy in the show who said, 'The show isn't working.' And he said, 'I'm going to come on and do my James Cagney in this scene.' We said, 'James Cagney isn't in this scene. You're a nun.' But he came on with a machine gun. He insisted on doing James Cagney. 'You see this, all right, OK, you gonna let me in your place, OK?' And we were hitting him, saying, 'Stop doing this, Steve.' We were arguing with each other on stage.

Oh God, there was some terrible, terrible stuff.

A few years later, I caught up with the man who ran the venue, and he said, 'Your stuff was shit.' At the time I thought it was kind of cutting-edge, but I think it was... cutting-edge shit. Except for this Jacques Cousteau sketch, which I didn't write. I did this bad French accent: 'After fourteen days on ze Calypso, we still 'ad not found sight of ze sea. Because we 'ad not left ze harbour. So we thought of pulling in ze anchor and zis was much better.'

And I sat there in a snorkel and flippers. 'Pierre would not go in with ze shark. So we pushed him in. It was vairy funny. He made some noises. We could not hear what he said.' It was recorded for the BBC, a show called *Aspects of the Fringe*, then they found out that Jacques Cousteau's

son had actually died and been eaten by a shark, so they cut it.

But that was the only redeeming thing – everything else was tripe.

I was nineteen when I took my show to Edinburgh in 1981. I went to Sheffield and said, 'OK, I didn't go to Cambridge but I can still go to the Edinburgh Festival, so let's go.' They said, 'We don't go.' I said, 'We must go. Everyone goes. All the universities go, don't they?' '*We* don't go. Some show lost money, so we don't go.'

So in February 1981 I hitch-hiked up to Edinburgh on my own

from the Tinsley Viaduct, then got to Newcastle and took a train up because it was getting late. I arrived at Waverley Station. Waverley was all lit up and it was fantastic. Someone I knew from school called Jimmy Ogglesby lived in a hall of residence and I was just going to turn up and say, 'Can I sleep on your floor?'. He was watching *Fawlty Towers* when I got there, which was ironic. And he said I could sleep on his floor.

I went down the fringe office the next day and said, 'I want to bring a show here: what do I do?' They said, 'Just fill in this, do that, get the money, anyone can come.' So I just begged, stole and borrowed money. I went up to Edinburgh before the show, blew all my exams out of the window and worked in a cafe, getting tips. I spent £100 on phone calls in the first four weeks, phoning people and asking them to come up and do the show. I roped my brother in, and people from school, just desperately trying to get people up to have a full contingent to do this show.

I did it on a wing and a prayer, and even though I didn't have enough confidence to do the show, I had a theory: if I assume I have the confidence, I'll tell everyone I'm doing it, and then people will come and we'll actually do it. Once we've done it, I'll have the confidence to do it again. It was some sort of weird positive thinking confidence mantra because I *had* to get there.

The show was just terrible, but we did it. The achievement

Our stuff was shit. At the time I thought it was kind of cutting-edge, but I think it was... cutting-edge shit

was getting there and performing it. I went up the next year with a better show, called *Sherlock Holmes Sings Country*. You had to make up stupid names. If you were doing a show, they'd say, 'Do you want to do this show?' I'd say, 'Yeah,' and they'd say, 'You can have the second week of college term. What's the name of the show?' We hadn't written it, so we just made up names. *A Pile of Haemorrhoids* was one. *Sherlock Holmes Sings Country* and *World War II: The Sequel*.

I was quite good at producing and getting people together. I was a terrible director. Writing, I was medium.

UPSTAGING AS A CAREER

I did a Sam Spade sleuth thing. It was all, 'I didn't know what I was gonna find but when I got there it was exactly as I had expected. I didn't know what to expect...' It was all a play on that.

We did *Ben Hur*. We had a female Ben Hur. It was bizarre. A lot of our stuff was written on the last day. I remember trying to get people to write stuff. We were all in the student union newspaper offices with typewriters and everyone kept messing around and I was saying, 'Write! We have

to do the show on Monday!' and it was Saturday, and we hadn't even written it. I just screamed at people all day: 'Write! We have to write!' And at the end of the day I looked at my typewriter and I'd written two lines.

After the first year at Sheffield I got kicked out. I didn't do any exams – I got 0 in Maths, having got three As before. I wrote nothing on the page. The professor said, 'There's nothing on the page!' I thought he was going to tear my head off, so I said, 'I didn't want to waste your valuable time.' And he said, 'Oh, that's very considerate.' So I got out of that one.

So I went down to London to find an agent and get known. I worked in the Fortune Theatre and did front of house on *The News Review Show*, in February 1983, for two weeks. I just thought, I'm not getting anywhere at this rate. I'll do another show at Sheffield. If you're a member of the student union at Sheffield, you become a life member and you can use their facilities. So I thought I'd do another show at Sheffield and take it up to Edinburgh again. That's when we took *Sherlock Holmes Sings Country*. And no-one came. No-one came to anything in Edinburgh. I thought it was the place to be discovered, but it isn't. You take your reputation from London up there and then they discover that you've already been discovered.

I had to go through all these different areas and styles to get my comedy to work. I haven't always done solo comedy. I used to be in a comedy group and only worked with other people. Then I was a double act because I couldn't get the other two of the comedy group down to London. And then I wanted to work more so I became a solo act.

World War II: The Sequel had 26 different characters. *The Great Escape* got into it: there was a part where everyone was digging a tunnel, and there was a gung-ho American sergeant called Sergeant Yo (he'd go, 'Yo!') – and a General Sir Largebrain Buttocks. I was in a stupid name phase.

But there was one nice scene which I really liked, based on the idea of the batman and the squadron leader thing. I think I was the batman. That was the part I really wanted to play, but I think I would probably have been better as the squadron leader. The squadron leader is going off on a mission and he's saying:

SQUADRON LEADER   All right, Bates, that's me all set. Tough mission today. I'll have to keep my wits about me to dodge the flack over Bremen. I might not be coming back on this one.

BATMAN   Yes, sir. I understand, sir.

And then the batman's going:

BATMAN   Sir, if you don't come back....can I – can I have your cuff links, sir?

SQUADRON LEADER   Well, I am coming back, don't worry Bates. I intend to return. I shall be coming back! Don't you worry about that!

BATMAN   But if you don't, you know, if there's a chance you're not coming back, sir, can I have your cuff links?

SQUADRON LEADER   Well, yes, all right, Bates, you've been a good man, very strong, very positive, so if I don't come back, then you can have my cuff links. All right, that's it. All right, I'm off to battle –

BATMAN   And also, sir, if you don't – can I have your shirts, sir? You've got these really nice shirts, they're very nice cotton, sir. Just in case. You don't want them to go to waste, do you, sir?

SQUADRON LEADER   No, that's true, but I am coming back.

BATMAN   But just in case, sir, if you don't come back. I just don't want them to be thrown out –

SQUADRON LEADER   All right, Bates. If I don't come back, you can have my shirts.

BATMAN   And the trousers, sir?

SQUADRON LEADER   What is it, Bates? Look, Bates! I tell you, I'm coming back.

BATMAN   I could find a good home for them, sir.

And he goes through an entire fucking load of possessions and really pisses the guy off. The squadron leader says:

SQUADRON LEADER   Right, I'm off now. Cheerio, Bates. I'll see you later.

He walks out the door and then about 30 seconds later he comes back in.

SQUADRON LEADER   Oh, Bates – I think I've left my...

Bates is standing there almost entirely dressed in his clothes (which are a bit big on him).

BATMAN   Oh hello, sir. I was just thinking. Your wife, sir. If you don't make it back...

Mondo Izzard

10 Downing Street, London. Eddie Izzard is just leaving after shaking hands with the Prime Minister.

'I said, "I hear you do interviews in French. I do my show in French," and he said, "Oh, that's good for Britain," and I said, "Yeah, I think it is." So that was the five minute chat we had. We didn't hang out and drive fast cars. That would have been interesting. We could have got off speeding tickets.'

Villains don't really worry me because I tend to think, fuck 'em, I'll live with the positive people. But I don't like Norman Tebbit. He was Thatcher's right-hand… killer. Ex-civil aviator. 'You are travelling on the airplane, the *SS Free Enterprise*…' He keeps having a go at me, just because I got involved in European politics. 'In my time, Churchill blah blah blah, and nowadays there are blokes going round with make-up on…' He has a big problem with that. He seems to think that being a transvestite isn't part of the mainstream. Why, I don't know, but he particularly picked up on the make-up area. But Thatcher wore make-up, and he was OK with that. Double standards.

I think him having a go at me is just a big thumbs-up really, a fantastic positive comment, but he keeps having a go in his column in the *Sun*. So,

he's a full-scale villain for me. He's just another one of the Little Englanders who have a problem with Europe. By not admitting that Europe's happening, they've made us be on the second string of Europe.

I don't believe there is a national sense of humour. I think there are several senses of humour in each country. In America, Archie Bunker and *The Simpsons* are quite a long way away from each other. Jim Davidson and *Python* – same country. *Python* is known in an alternative way in America, France and Denmark. I sold out in Denmark before I got there because the Danish comedians knew me from coming over to London. I've said on occasions, 'There's good comedy in the rest of Europe. Don't be stupid and think, oh, there's never going to be Danish comedy, because they're going to come over and do it in English.' In music, we didn't think Abba was going to happen, and Kraftwerk, and Björk and Daft Punk. We had an economy, then Germany came along. We thought we were good at football, then the other Europeans got really good...

I am fascinated by politics but I'm not hugely involved in it. Well, I'm not involved in it at all. With the Europe issue, which I am very interested in, there's that line of people saying, 'Who are *you* to talk?' The only platform I have on Europe thing is I'm positive about it and I'm going to go there and do gigs all over the Continent, in different languages.

I did my act in French in Paris, and there's an enormous sense of pride about talking for two hours for six days in a different language. That should get you an A-level or something, just because it scared the shit out of me. I found it so difficult. I've been into all the psychology on language. My thing was to communicate first and worry about the grammar second. The best way to do it the first time is to get pissed. You become more fluent that way. And my French got fantastically better over the six days when I performed in Paris.

The *NME* came and reviewed it and unfortunately they didn't know enough French, which made it very difficult to review.

I've seen Swedish comedians and I've said to them, 'I think you're very good, but I'm not sure. I don't speak Swedish.'

With stand-up comedy, I feel we've been held back. I remember on British television, some kids were asked, 'What's the best comedy?' and they all said, 'American comedy,' because they see the best of American comedy, they don't see the dross. I've always hated this thing that our comedy can't cut it. It fucking *can* – we've just got to get it to the USA. It's good that Lee Evans is doing his thing. *Mr Bean*'s making a lot of money, *Ab Fab* has cut through.

In Europe, the little Englanders feel they're losing sovereignty but I feel we're gaining the greater sovereignty of Europe. If they're worried about losing power we should get in there so we don't lose it all – and perhaps we'd be gaining more power. We have some positive ideas in Britain that could happen all over Europe.

I used to have images of places like Blackpool – amusement arcades and mainstream comics with gold watches saying, 'My wife, my wife, on and on and on...' Then I played Blackpool and I don't suppose initially I got a load of Blackpool people there. I got kids from Lancaster University coming down and I thought 'Hey, Blackpool! Yeah! A fun time!' I went to Preston and that was OK. Stornaway! Ullapool! It's a fantastic way to see the UK.

I feel I've played more places in Scotland than most Scottish comedians. The interesting thing is that there used to be the King Of Scots as opposed to the King of Scotland, and all the clan thing which was kind of aboriginal – not linked to the land *per se*, but more this big mistrust of one another. So you go to Ullapool in the Highlands of Scotland having just left Stornoway and they say, 'Stornoway? Weird bunch of people up there.' Go to Orkney and they go, 'Ullapool? Weird bunch of people there.' Go to Shetland – 'Orkney? Weird bastards...'

So everyone sort of distrusts each other. I played this place called The Ceilidh Place in Ullapool. It's a fishing village and there's this little alternative enclave there. I did it acoustically, no mike, no nothing, to 70 people, which was great fun. I had my two hands free for the first time in ages. And it was a great gig. I was an English guy playing the Highlands of Scotland, which is not exactly a pro-English bastion, and afterwards this SNP woman was saying, 'We were ready to kill you.'

But I was in black PVC trousers, an orange Gaultier jacket and lipstick: 'I'm not really English, I'm just from outer space.' So you actually get the international passport to places, from being so weird you don't really seem to be from anywhere. You just seem to be a universal person, or so weird that you've just come back round and joined up with... everything.

I want to play Moscow. I should go on the internet and say, 'Hello, Moscow. If anyone from Moscow reads this we're looking for interesting groovy places to play. Have you been to Moscow? Are you from Moscow?' It's just like making a local phone call.

It excites me, this idea of going round and playing all these different places in Europe. I want to do all these bonkers tours, because there's only any interest in the press if you've got an angle. The music press is so linked to whether you're going to smash places up, or say everyone's a cunt or whatever, something that has a good rock'n'roll spin on it. And I can't be bothered to smash up hotel rooms. I've got to live in them.

I like the idea of going out and doing the Spitfire Village Hall Tour. And

I don't believe there is a national sense of humour. I think there are several senses of humour in each country

I'm in the unique position of not having to check with my bass player or my guitarist: I can just say, 'Spitfires and village halls.' I can learn to fly, get a Spitfire, go to all these little airstrips that were used in the Second World War, fly round Britain and play all these village halls. I don't quite know how I'd get from the airfield to the village hall – I'd really need to have an E-type Jag there. And have it covered on telly. It'd be fantastic. Or a biplane if a Spitfire's too difficult. Two seats in the back, cameraman. I think some of the Mark VI Spitfires had seats in the back. I had this Spitfire game and it had Mark VIs. It was called Achtung Spitfire, of course.

My head's stuck in some sort of Second World War thing. I don't know if kids born in the seventies are so obsessed with the war, but I did get a drawing done by a kid who must have been twelve at the time, and it was a US warship and a German tank in a plane attack. I thought, how odd to be drawing *that* scene. It was odd in the sixties and seventies to be running around going, 'You're the Germans, you're the British.' The Vietnam War didn't impinge on that at all.

I was still reading those little war magazines. I loved all those. And the film *Iron Cross*. I was talking to Christopher Hampton, who directed *Carrington* and *The Secret Agent*, about the film, *Iron Cross*. I said, 'I like that *Iron Cross*.' It's a Sam Peckinpah film, about the Russian Front. It's got James Coburn as a sergeant who was busted down from an officer, and he's the can-do kind of guy. A Prussian officer turns up who wants to get an Iron Cross. And this sergeant has an Iron Cross. But Christopher Hampton hated it... it's not his kind of film.

Saving Private Ryan starts on the beaches of Normandy. I just keep going back there. My dad took me when I was a kid. I don't know what it is; I just feel I should have been there to *do a bit*. It was just something I wanted to be involved in. It's the big male tomboy part of me.

Doing comedy in France, I just link up with the audience who like surreal comedy. They had the whole surrealist movement of art in Europe and it wasn't for everyone, it wasn't a mainstream thing. I would love to tour round France. Toulouse and Tours and Lyons. I sometimes find it hard to believe that people actually work there, and that it's not just shopowners selling quaint knickknacks. Going to school in France must be as boring as going to school here, and there's unemployment and strikes, but I still haven't totally got that into my head. France to me is like an entire country designed as a holiday place for people to visit.

I like French music. I like getting very generically French stuff. There's a lot of French fifties, probably classic folk-like tunes. I hate that thing in

film or telly where whenever the story happens to cut to France, it's sud-denly – *nah dee dio* – a fucking accordion… It's nice to hear the real French songs. I was in a restaurant where they were all singing them: 'Roll Out The Barrel' is a European song. '*Je suis un da da, da da da da da…*' And there's a German one, '*Ich bin da da da, da da da da da…*' War songs. Nazi war songs were also communist war songs. Like Lili Marlene was a British and a German song. The music just sort of went around and everyone changed the lyrics. 'We'll kill those British every-where' was 'We'll kill those Germans everywhere' in our version.

Like football. There's that wordless song they do in Europe: '*O-layyy, O-lay, O-lay, O-layyy, O-layyy, O-layyy.*' It just goes on and on and on. No real words. Words are too complicated.

France is a particular favourite place, because of this thing that I believe the Izzards were Huguenots 500 years ago. I've researched this a fair bit. I did a *Clive James Show* with the Two Fat Ladies and one of them said, 'Oh, Izzard, that's a Huguenot name,' and I said, 'Hold up, this is what I've heard,' and she said, 'Oh yeah, I've read it all up and the Izzard name is definitely Huguenot.' Isard is the French version of it and someone said there's loads of Issards in the Pyrenees. Antoine De Caunes told me there's

a mountain and a little village called Les Issards and an Isard is actually a mountain goat. So the Isards were goat herders or maybe they were goats. The spelling changed, as spellings did then.

Anne Boleyn spelt her name seventeen different ways. I don't know how you do that with Anne Boleyn – 'Bolin, Buleen, Byelin' but it must have been double Ls and double Ys.

There's that wordless song they do in Europe: 'O-layyy, O-lay, O-lay, O-layyy, O-layyy, O-layyy.' It just goes on and on and on. No real words. Words are too complicated

So they would have written it down Isard and when they were kicked out of France with all the other Protestants, the English would have said, 'You want to be Izzard; you want to put a Z in there.' We found an Izzard in the 1700s spelled Iszard, which sounds like the missing link.

We're everywhere. There's an Isard County in Arkansas and if you look up 'Izzard' on the internet you get a load of stories about some senator who lost an election battle recently.

Apparently, the reason the Protestants were kicked out of France was because they worked on saints' days. And at the time in France there were 200 saints' days, so they were making a ton of cash because the Catholics didn't work on saints' days. It's economics, which affects everything in the end. The Pink Pound – gay business was brought into society by the establishment because there was disposable cash being spent. Huguenots were kicked out because they were making too much money.

In Europe now there are many new nations, which is the weird by-product of Europe separating out. But I think that's OK, as long as you draw a line somewhere and it's not, 'There's six people here and we're going to be a new nation.' That's too much. I'm pleased about Wales and Scotland having their own assemblies. Northern Ireland – we have a messy historical

situation due to the English sending settlers in there. We'll see.

When you're in America and you're hanging out with someone from Canada or Australia, you suddenly feel, 'God, you're my next door neighbour,' because there are so many cultural links. But when you're in Britain, you feel, 'Australia's miles away!' But the Canadians and the Australians have a whole bunch of sayings and television programs that are the same as in Britain. They'd know about *Doctor Who* and *Thunderbirds*, and all those kids programmes.

I suppose there is a more earthy, working culture in Australia. They swear more: 'Bollocks to the Queen. She can fuck off as far as I'm concerned, the bloody Queen.' And that's just their Prime Minister.

There's a ton of Canadian comedians who almost control comedy in America. They've got Dan Aykroyd, the big large guy who died, John Candy,

Mike Myers, Jim Carrey, all the guys in *Kids In The Hall*... there was a bunch. They seem to have a route in to America. Maybe they have some sort of spin in comedy that's slightly different to the American thing.

Nelson Mandela, he's done great. Just because the moves he made have been very generous after 26 years in prison. He hasn't started stringing people up. I think the truth commission he set up has been having some problems, though. White people come along and say 'I did wrong' and get let off. It was an idea not of being vengeful but of getting everything out in the open. Punishment seems to be not specifically attached to it. Pik Botha or one of the Botha lads was refusing to turn up.

No, Mandela's just done great. It made me feel really good to be in a world where he can get out of prison and the whole government can turn

over and you don't have this vast hellish killing spree which the Afrikaaners enacted, even when there was no war officially going on.

So I love that. I want to go and play there. I want to play in Soweto and the groovy paces in South Africa. I've been advised that I shouldn't go round playing all these various places, because I'm laying seeds but it will take ages for flowers to grow. Apparently, in Europe, if I play Paris and Berlin, they're the places that Europe respects. It's not that they don't respect London, but it's English-speaking so – fuck it, you know? Just imagine trying to do it in German in Berlin and French in Paris. I got the French up to speed but the German I need to work on – '*Das Auto fur den Flughafen bitte. Haben Sie eine kleine Nachtmusik?*'

It's interesting that Seinfeld did a gig in Reykjavik. I've already done that. And he started doing a bit of a European tour.

I think what draws me to the Europe thing is the idea of, 'Hey, what can come out of the biggest melting pot in the world?' 500 million people, we've just got to melt a bit. The idea of doing shows in Paris and Germany, in Spain and Italy, and in those languages as well, that's melting in action.

My genes are already mixed up. My mother's side was German, if you go back two generations. Go back about fifteen generations to the Huguenots – 'Izzard' was from the Pyrenees. That's a Spanish-French kind of thing. So I'm the perfect European. If everyone explored their ancestry, they'd probably find the same. I like this mixing-up of the genes.

The English all hate the French, for some reason. Why? It's such casual lazy thinking, such casual bigotry

I was on this programme about the French. The English all hate the French, for some reason. They were interviewing people in the street and they all said, 'Yeah, I hate the French. Why? Because they're so... French. They're so full of themselves...' It's such casual lazy thinking, such casual bigotry. And you go to France, and it's beautiful. Well, it's just as crap and as beautiful as Britain can be or Germany, or Holland.

I love languages but I have this weird block about seeing films with subtitles, which may explain why nobody in France laughed when I did my Sean Connery impression. It was part of the show, and I did the show in Paris in French. And Sean Connery was Noah in the last show so he was going, '*Sh'ai fabrique un arche, ah, Dieu. Vous voulez quelque-chose de?*' and James Mason's going, '*Oui, je voulaihhh un arche...*' And it was great doing this, '*Esh-que, ah, vous voulez shuh couchez avec moi?*'

But then this French guy said to me three months later, 'Look, you realise that he's dubbed in France and so we have no idea what he sounds like,' so it was a complete waste of time. But a lot of my audience were English speakers who had come to Paris from Britain or somewhere else – Australia – so they got it. I thought it was beautiful – '*Je suis ishi depuis, ah, douzhe ans*' – but the French just didn't get it.

Street Performing Man

New York. Eddie Izzard and his reviews. 'I was reviewed here as a human search engine, which I really like,' he says happily. 'It's all about obsessive detail on crap. My website, *www.izzard.com*, has just won second best website from *Yellow Pages*. It's good. People log on and say what they want. It's had 6000 hits in six weeks. I think it might be eight people just constantly logging in.'

He looks at some photographs and sighs. 'You just can't look like a tomboy with a powder puff in your hand,' he says.

There's a place called Terschelling, where they have the Oerol festival. It's in north west Holland and it's an island. It gets taken over by the kids from Rotterdam and Amsterdam and I played it in the late eighties. It's amazing. These were the street performing years – it would have been '87, '88, '89. If you're a student of life or comedy, you must go. It's like a rock festival and a comedy festival combined.

You do stuff in the streets. The police came into our show and performed with us. It was drugs all round us. Everyone was doing dope drops, where instead of giving you money at the end of shows, they'd give you hash. So we said, 'Look, we've run out of hash, can we get some hash?' and we wouldn't start the show until someone came up and gave us some. This

was at the end of the festival and all the kids were in this fenced-off area waiting for a ferry to get back home.

So the promoter said, 'Go down and play there and I'll bung you some money and make it nice and then the people waiting for the boats don't get too bored.' So I was performing with some friends, and then the police turned up in their car so we thought, OK, we'll play with the police. And we shouted, 'Run away, the police are after us.' And then we thought, where can we go with this now? Let's go round and talk to them.

Instead of trying to make things happen your way, you use what is happening. You sense it's going to happen and then say, 'I am making this happen'

And we wandered round and talked to them as though we were the police, looking at the car and asking them to wind down the window. And I knew I had to say something, so I ad-libbed in Dutch – which was for me brilliant, because I don't speak Dutch. I said the one Dutch phrase I know, 'Have you got the time?' Big laugh. They told me the time and then they put their siren on, so we ran, and they chased us in the police car. We were all just playing around. It was fucking great.

You can do *anything* in street performing. I started one show just lying on the ground asleep and when a crowd was there I started the show. It's great for learning how to perform on the street. A lot of people seize up. Now, when people come up to me on the street, I back off a bit, but if I get talking to them it's OK. Once you've learned to perform on the street, you can do amazing things.

Once I did a two-hour street show, and this crazy guy came along and walked into the show. He was talking bollocks and I was talking bollocks. Street shows can be wonderful things. There's a guy called J. J. Waller from Brighton, who would use the clouds in his show. We all used to watch the clouds, because it kept raining on us, so you're quite aware of the weather. When it was cloudy, and he could see the sun was about to come out from behind a cloud, he'd say, 'And can we have the lights up, please?' and then the sun would come out.

It was beautiful. Instead of trying to make things happen your way, you use what is happening. You sense it's going to happen and then say, 'I am making this happen.' They know you haven't done it, but they like your timing.

I used a fire once. There was a fire in a building in Princes Street in Edinburgh, and as the fire engines approached, I was saying, 'This is my fire. I set this up earlier. I set incendiary devices to go off and the guy driving the fire engine, that's Steve at the front, and that's Geoff, and that's Bernie, and we put the fire on the second floor...' And the audience knew I was pissing about – or they hoped I was pissing about. I was going, 'Shit, I hope no-one's dying in there.' It was kind of scary that I could play with it.

At the start of the Edinburgh Festival, they have this parade of floats and stuff and they invite dignitaries, generals and the mayor of something and ... someone from *Star Trek*. They had a load of limos at the back

of this gallery, and all the street performers were waiting for the parade to go by so the crowd would split up.

I used to set up these tea cosies. A penguin, a duck, a hippo and a pig, which I'd bought in the Covent Garden General Store. I'd put them on the ground and they'd look stupid. If you do things very slowly and with a lot of concentration, people will just watch. Even if it's a packet of cigarettes, people will watch you do it because you're taking so much time over it. And that was just to get a crowd.

So I was doing that and all these limos were there and I was saying, 'In a minute a few people are going to come through that door. They're all friends of mine. One guy's dressed up as a general. That's Steve. He always does that. He always stays rigidly in character, he never pulls out. You can say, "Hey Steve! Wave hello!" and he won't do it, he'll stay in character.'

And I set this thing up, which the audience knew was bullshit, but it was a nice scenario. You couldn't lose on it. The general would come out and you could go, 'Steve! Steve!' and he'd ignore you. 'Look at that! Look at that attention to detail. He will not break out of character, will you Steve? I can poke him, I can hit him with a bat, I can hit him with a fluffy pig, he will not change...' And it was no-lose because he either came with me, which would be bizarre, or he would stay as a general, which would feel like it had worked. Trouble was the drivers saw what I was doing and moved their limos.

Imposing scenarios is a beautiful thing. People would walk through a show and I would say, 'This is Janine, and Mr Simpson here, they walk through like this, at this diagonal, and then they change clothes and come back disguised as two different people.' Later in the show, two other people might go by – 'There they go! There they go again, Janine and Mr Simpson there!'

What I like about street performing is that it's ungraded. In stand-up or rock'n'roll there's a very strict hierarchy. The biggest band headlines and the smaller one goes on first. But with street performers, because there's no hierarchy and it's an open-door policy, anyone can get on, so you could be a beginner going on after someone who's been doing it for twenty years. So if you turn up as an average punter you can't tell what the show's going to be like.

Ironically, street performers have no street credibility even though they're on the bloody street. We were considered completely non-street credible.

So, out of street performing came the ability to play. And these days I have microphone technique. I use those little mikes that clip on and I also use the traditional hand-held ones. I find the hand held mikes are fine, but it can be difficult. For crucifixion scenes, mainly.

When Virgin Atlantic were doing their first flights, they had in-flight entertainers. My partner Rob and I auditioned for it with a knife-throwing act. We just showed them the knives and they said, 'I don't think so.' I think we sat in someone's office, some product manager-type person, saying, 'Well, we get a lot of mess. Escaping from a woolly jumper and making a bowl of cornflakes disappear by eating them.' The people in the front row wouldn't have been happy. It would'nt have worked. Knives going through the air – *zzzing*! I didn't think it would be a good act on a plane, but it was the only act we did.

Virgin have this section called Upper Class on their planes. I thought First Class sounded bad enough, but *Upper Class* ... you might as well call it Aristocracy. I think they should just call it Fabulous.

I'm into improvisation. I do a show called *One Word Improv*, which does get a mixed reaction. But I like the total release. It's like your mind is on fire out there. You stand on stage and you say crap and they take your crap and build on it. Often in the voice of James Mason:

'Ah, my legs are covered in jam. My brother comes with sausages from afar overseas. I have not seen him in nigh on seven years now and... my heart bleeds internally.'

'Sir, the doctor is here for your heart. Your brother is seen on the port bow of the ship and whatever you said earlier is also in place.'

'But! You, Carruthers, you plot against me!'

'I don't plot against you, sir. I'm your dentist.'

'That's... true, but you dentists have always been against me. You hated me ever since I passed the Dentists Act of 1947, where... all dentists were forced to be shot against their will.'

'Yes, sir.'

You just go quite fast through this stuff and the others come back with more shit, sometimes in the voice of James Mason:

'I have come! I am your brother!'

Ironically, street performers have no street credibility even though they're on the bloody street. We were considered completely non-street credible

And the best bit was to take the rubbish they had fed you earlier and re-incorporate it:

'I am your brother! I have turned back.'

'Ah, brother! There was a reason why you weren't here, wasn't there? I can't remember what it was, though.'

Some people said *One Word* was bitty, because it was stop/start, but I think you have to lower your expectations slightly because it is improv, and some of it is... *shit*. We started reincorporating characters – a technique from stand-up where you introduce a character and keep bringing them back. I started threading stuff through like my music teacher, Mrs Badcrumble, for example, and Gunter Heimlich, of the Heimlich manoeuvre. But the improv – I loved it.

Neil Mullarkey was in *One Word* and he was rehearsing for a sketch show at the Lyric, Hammersmith, all day, and he would turn up and do improv. He'd get there and he'd be tired and miserable. But as soon as he came on stage, within about 30 seconds, when he got his first joke in,

and got his first laugh, he'd be on again. We used to lay bets on how long it would take before he became cheerful again.

Then we kept trashing all the chairs because we were trying to be The Who of comedy, where instead of trashing expensive equipment we'd be destroying cheap furniture.

It took me two years to get into the Comedy Store. A man called Kim Kinney used to book the acts. He never normally went to other gigs, but by chance he kept turning up at my early gigs, just as I was going down the toilet, to reaffirm the fact that I was the worst stand-up in the history of stand-up.

Three times at the Comedy Store I went on after Jerry Sadowitz. They used to have a very bad policy at the Store where the beginner would go on after the headliners. They would close with Jerry's stuff which was brilliant and unsettling at the same time. High energy, in your face, blistering stand-up for 20 minutes. People were just stunned and screaming and shouting and laughing or whatever. And then the open spot would go on – 'Hi! Got a sofa. Uh. Yeah. Fish are dangerous, aren't they?' They'd just die.

I just kept going on after Jerry. It's so weird that he likes my stuff now.

I always thought that the Pythons could do stand-up, but they wouldn't do it now because they'd have to go through such hell to learn the technique of doing it. I used to do what they did, playing a role where you're inside the character – but when you do stand-up, you have to learn to play *yourself*. And I pushed to learn that.

I could do all these stupid voices and put all the costumes on and whatever, but I couldn't do *me*. So my big success through street performing was learning how to get me out there and saying, 'Hi, look, we're going to do this, blah blah blah...' and that was the real me talking. I never did characters on the street but then when I went indoors again, I had my own persona and I had the old characters through sketch comedy and it all came together and became the thing I do now.

The act began to evolve. Early stuff like *I was raised by wolves*. That was my first 'single'. And *Le singe est sur la branche* was my second 'single'. They were all singles that came out without an album. *Le singe* is from my old orange French textbook, and my old French teacher actually corrected me about this later, because I used to say, 'Le singe est dans l'arbre', which means, 'The monkey is *inside* the tree.'

Then this idea came to me about the sitcom – *Cows* – which was kind of like *The Day of the Triffids*, where a big meteor goes overhead and all the plants start moving. I just imagined some sort of meteorite happening and all the cows starting talking and walking round and becoming another social group in society and getting the vote. And that was *Cows*, which eventually was filmed as a pilot for a sitcom. People thought it was a funny idea, but I was always worried that it talked up a good pitch but might not work as a programme. In the end it *didn't* come off, but that's fine because I don't think it's the end of that story, and it can be picked up. It can be done in Claymation and I can do voices and be part of it.

Cows is in a holding position. Initially I'd seen Alexei Sayle playing a mouse in a balaclava – 'Whoopee, I'm a mouse, do you have any ketchup?' – where he was a man in a mouse costume, and I thought I'd do the cows like that. But as it went along the production values got higher and I thought, we can't just do that. We've got to make them

more *cowlike*. Then we tried to do a *Planet of the Apes* thing. I suppose in the end, apes were two-legged with the face not changing much between human and ape, and they had a film budget and we had a television budget and we were going for four legs with long faces. And with all the prosthetics, there was a loss of the detail you get from the face...

I think *Cows* could still work but it's got to be animation.

Then I did my TV film *Lust for Glorious*, which was an exaggerated, shithead version of me. I managed to re-enact the fight I had in Cambridge. I'm wearing PVC trousers and a black PVC top so I'm like a bigger Emma Peel. Big set of heels. And at the end I get into an Aston Martin and drive off. I liked the idea of the huge ego trip of it, only – this time I was gonna win the fight!

The whole vibe of the film is, 'I wanna be big in America, I wanna be bigger than McDonalds.' It has the American agent character in it – 'Eddie, we like what you do, you're gonna make it big in America, but you gotta lose this make-up thing, it's very confusing. We wanna see you in cars, driving around, having fights...' And it became like the rock band video. We took bits of a Bon Jovi video, *Destination Anywhere*.

They had a whole scene – trying to make it more interesting – where Jon Bon Jovi is acting out scenes with Demi Moore, and it doesn't come off. He's got a scene where he's sitting round talking with a group of women and there's a black woman there and some babies and he's saying, 'Sometimes I just want to go off on a motorbike and it really is 'Destination Anywhere.' 'Wherever I stop, that's where I hang out – *man*.'

So we did exactly the same scene. In *Lust for Glorious* we're standing outside a room in Soho and there's my publicist there and another woman, and everyone's just agreeing with me. There's a little black kid as well. We just told him, 'Stand there and look bored.'

And I was saying, 'Yeah, I just wanna drive in a car. One tank of petrol, just drive.' I was just trying to ad-lib all those cliches. 'One tank, yeah. I just wanna live til I die. No longer.' Immense bullshit.

I went to France. The guy playing my manager in the video said, 'Where were you born?' I said, 'Aden, Yemen.' He said, 'That's no good, that's Arabs. No-one knows what they do over there. Do the French thing. You were born in France.' 'I can't say I was born in France.' But I went into a fish shop and just talked to the guy about the weather in French and in the film they dubbed on a whole conversation – 'Remember me?' 'Yes, indeed I do. It is young Edouard Izzard.'

I did the film *The Secret Agent*, which was very different. Christopher Hampton came and saw my stand-up and was very positive. He gave me the part of the shithead Russian diplomat, Vladimir. The book is quite dark. It's about despair really, and so, you know…dark. Robin Williams, Gerard Depardieu, Bob Hoskins, Patricia Arquette. They're all in it.

Most scenes in films are a page long – the scene they filmed on the first day was six pages long, and I had most of the dialogue. In a Russian accent. With things like, 'You purport to be, uh, an anarchist, uh, a revolutionary. You're rather corpulent for an anarchist, aren't you?' All this to Bob Hoskins. Bob Hoskins was going, 'Don't worry about dialogue.'

And I was saying, 'Fuck! I've got truckloads of it!' Lines like, 'I want to do something to create an outrage... to attack the fetish of the hour.'

It seemed to turn out all right. I had some moments. Nice staring in the mirror and turning to the left. At one point, there's me, Peter Vaughan, who was Mr Big in *Porridge* – 'Fletcher. Fletch. Hello Fletch. Want you to do something for me' 'Oh yeah, Grouty, what's that?' – and Gerard Depardieu. All speaking French to each other.

I remember me pushing this tape into Robin Williams' hand and him watching it. I had this routine about when doctors take your blood pressure I said they're not *actually* taking your blood pressure, they're operating a jumpy spider behind your back. Stupid stuff like that. And then they filmed a scene where Robin Williams plays a professor and he has gelignite strapped to him. He sells dynamite to anarchists but the police can never arrest him because he'll just explode himself and take everyone with him. And his hand's always on this squeeze-pump detonator.

Robin came up to me afterwards and said, 'Ha! Jumpy spider!' I thought, 'Wow – he's been watching my video! '

I think I should have been intimidated when I did *The Secret Agent* but I'd just come from doing *Edward II* on stage, so I felt more backed up to go on and do a film. In *Edward II*, I played this gay king who dies with a poker up the backside after being held captive in a pool of shit. So after *that*, you're kind of more relaxed about acting anything.

In *Edward II*, I played this gay king who dies with a poker up the backside after being held captive in a pool of shit. So after *that*, you're relaxed about acting anything

In *The Avengers* I only had these little scenes with Sean Connery. It wasn't, 'You talkin' to me? You talkin' to me? I don't see anybody else here.' It was more like, 'You're obviously not talking to me as I have no lines.'

I didn't quite have enough to get my teeth into. They said, 'We'll put some more lines in,' and gave me three more lines and I said, 'No, no more lines, we'll take 'em out.' Because Steve McQueen used to take lines out. I think my character was expected to say a few lines – stuff like 'Don't you do that, John Steed.' But it was more powerful if I wasn't saying *anything*. So I thought, I'll just stare at people and be enigmatic in some way. Some sort of silent guy who stares at people, hits them, chews gum and controls killer bees...

I'm in the promo advert, as well, hanging from wires for about a second, and Uma Thurman has a go at me. She beats the shit out of me.

There's me and Shaun Ryder in *The Avengers* going round with Uzi machine guns. Shaun would very often be getting in straight from the studio and he could go straight to work because he just looked like a heavy. We sat in a Mini chatting away and then it would be, 'Oh, we've got to shoot Uzis now' and they would go, 'All right, guys, here's some more Uzis loaded up.' 'Thanks.'

Shaun was driving but the wheels weren't touching the ground, there was a lorry dragging it along so when the lorry turned we turned. There was a motorbike and sidecar shooting film from the side. The stunt arranger was in charge of everything, and he just pointed at Shaun to shoot. Then I started shooting and spent shells were coming out the side of my gun and hitting Shaun on the head, so I had to get the thing right out of the window so the shells didn't hit him.

And there was Uma Thurman and Ralph Fiennes in an E-type Jag and we were shooting at them from a Mini Cooper. Great fun. We were driving

down an embankment and I was controlling killer bees...

It's odd. Initially I thought I was just going to do comedy so I stopped envisaging action-hero type roles. But I think I can now spin it round... I'd like to have played Alan Rickman's role in *Die Hard*. There's a great bit where he does an American accent – 'Oh God, oh God, don't kill me!' We really didn't expect *that*.

Stand-up comedy and film acting are very different. There's a certain purity about comedy. If you want to be original in stand-up, you just talk about your own sad life and people go, 'Oh, that's interesting.' So you can be as sad as you want – 'You know, I can't tie my shoelaces. I never was able to tie my shoelaces and I *still* can't tie my shoelaces, because I was attacked by shoelaces when I was a kid.' And people will love it. Whereas you wouldn't do that in a film. Unless you're playing the weird shoelace guy.

But films are great. I'd like to do a medium role now, rather than just hanging around. I'm talking about trailers. There's a fantastic thing about trailers. If you've being given a trailer on set, you go 'Ooh! A trailer!' Then you start looking around and you start getting trailer envy: '*That* guy, I think my part's bigger than his, I've got more lines than he has, and he's got a bigger trailer than me. He's got an extra sink!' And you start going around telling yourself, 'Just calm down, it's only a film. Forget this trailer thing... Oh, there's the star. How big's the star's trailer? Oh, a big old trailer, with a bit that comes out at the side...'

If you're working on an independent film with a smaller budget, you're

in a good trailer on some days and in a smaller one if there's a lot of people doing the scene. And you're like, 'Oh shit, who's in *my* trailer?' Sometimes you get trailer guilt, when you're in a trailer and someone else who should be on level pegging with you is in just a changing-room. It's so nothing to do with anything, but you start getting kind of fixated by it. You phone your agent – 'Is my trailer supposed to have a window in the top?'

And they do everything for you in films. You want a cup of tea and they'll send someone to get a cup of tea for you. And then you have to try to say, 'No, *I'll* get the cup of tea. No! I'll get it.' And in the end you just go, 'Yes, cup of tea, and I want *this*, and I want *that*...' You can also say, 'I want some Hula Hoops,' so someone is sent off in a car to get Hula Hoops. But to be honest I don't think I've done that. I've never ordered Hula Hoops on a film set.

Sometimes I've said, 'I need a massage,' and in the studio there might be someone there who does massage, but I'm happy to buy massages myself. Massage and free wigs is all I ask for on a film set. I tend to go round sort of not stretched when I'm doing these things and I store it all in my shoulders but I'm trying to be calmer. Doing *Velvet Goldmine*, I would do scenes and at the end of the day I would just be very tight in my back because I would be trying so hard to get it right. When I do stand-up it's a lot more comfortable. I just go, 'Hey! So... there's fish everywhere... missus.'

There's a lot of freedom in stand-up, because usually it isn't being recorded. You do what you want, and if you fuck up, you fuck up.

Initially I thought I was just going to do comedy so I stopped envisaging action-hero type roles. But I think I can now spin it round...

Sex, Crime and Space

**London: a sunny afternoon. Eddie Izzard comes into a cafe. A man
gets up to say hello. It's the great Jerry Sadowitz, Britain's most
abusive comedian. He shakes hands with Eddie. 'Bloody funny guy,'
he says.**

**Later, a girl comes up to Eddie's table. She looks embarrassed
as she says, 'I know you'll hate this but I think you're the most
wonderful person and I'm so glad you exist and I wish there were
more men like you.'**

**'Bizarre thing,' Eddie says afterwards. 'I don't really know how to
deal with those compliments.' He does not look displeased, however.**

I want things to be kind of sexy because I feel particularly *not* sexy.
Even though I'd like to. When I was a teenager, I felt even less sexy.
I had a poor sexual self-image. I would have gone into rock'n'roll.
When punk was happening, there was this guy at school who was deeply
into punk and he said, 'Look, they're just asking anyone to send in records.'
So we recorded this track and sent it in, and it was put on this compilation
of crazy people. Fuck knows what it was called: it would have been 1979.
It was this kid called Matthew Wright who just knew so much about it and
was so interested in getting into it. I've been trying to locate him ever since.

I went to see Pulp and I met up with one kid who was from school. He's now running this snowboard company. I had a conversation with him in the toilets. He said, 'You taught me the paradiddle on the drums.' I went, 'Oh, right.' I meet so many people that for about 30 seconds, it was really difficult to remember. So I thought, I must have been there and said, 'I can do a paradiddle' and done one, so I said, 'All right,' and went off.

And then I met him again the same evening and somehow we got back into this conversation and he said, 'No, we were at school. I'm Mark Adams.' I went 'Fucking hell, man.' It just totally blew me away. I was like, 'Wow!' Because loads of people from school went off to work in the City so I was pleased to meet someone who got into something interesting. But, yeah, I taught him drums.

At school, my way of getting out of marching round the place was to march round the place ... playing the drums. I wanted to be a drummer. I had the drums that were at an angle – they had to be at an angle because you can't walk otherwise. They had all these standard military riffs that they were into, and me and this other guy, Chris Bucknall, who played the tenor drum, went out on to the school pitch one day – it was some kind of sponsored thing – and we made up a bunch of weirder drum combinations. I wanted to do that, and I became the silver drummer. You got these black sticks with solid silver ends and you would do the solo piece.

Rock'n'roll seemed far too sexy for me, but comedy was a way of getting girls. If you could make people laugh, you were popular at school. A lot of people definitely get into it as a way of getting off with people.

Rock'n'roll is great for that, and comedy is just a little way behind.

Being in a sketch comedy group was amazing, but it's a kind of unwieldly, difficult group. I used to be in a group of four people, and then I was in a group of two – and just to get the two together was difficult. We used to have meetings about deciding when we were going to have meetings to decide when we were going to change stuff and put new stuff in. But as a solo it's very free-wheeling: there's a great freedom. And touring is brilliant.

I like the idea of putting myself

in situations and being more than an observer. I wanted to be like Steve McQueen in *Bullitt*. Instead of acting it and being crap, I thought, Let's try and *do* it, and put myself in dangerous situations.

But I was walking through Times Square in New York and this guy was looking at me and shouting, 'Fuckin' faggot!' And I was going, '*You're* a fuckin' faggot.' I shout whatever they shout at me. So some people were going, 'I saw you on telly,' and other people were going, 'Fucking faggot,' and one person said, 'Are you funny? Say funny! Say funny now!' I was saying, 'I'm expensive, I'll only do it for $10,000.' 'Tell me funny now!' 'Give me $10,000 and I'll be funny'. I thought, If he gets that money out, I'd better be funny...

And I could feel the aggression coming off those people. I'm no good at fighting but I just can't stick it if people shout shit. And it can happen anywhere. If I'm in Leicester Square at night, I'll get it.

When I was younger, I broke into Pinewood Studios, I broke into Elstree Studios, I broke into the TV room at school... and I stole make-up. Yeah. The things I needed to get, I would get. *Allure* magazine just gave me 55 lipsticks to try out. That's a great irony for me, having stolen lipstick from Bexhill-On-Sea Boots The Chemist when I was fifteen. I got caught, but I was too young to go to prison. I didn't want to buy it because I thought someone might say, 'Why are you, a boy, buying make-up? You must be a transvestite.' It could be embarrassing. So I thought, 'I'll steal it. Then no-one will know... except me and the judicial system.'

Rock'n'roll seemed far too sexy for me, but comedy was a way of getting girls. If you could make people laugh, you were popular at school

My stepmother was in the SAS. She was in the signals. It was '44 – the desert war was over and the SAS were all being dropped into Normandy, preparing for invasion. They don't light fires, they just lie low. When they send messages it was 30 seconds and then out. So you have to *get* that message straight away. They can't go, 'Sorry, what was that again?'

So there were about nine signal operators seconded into the SAS and my stepmother was one of them. She can talk in Morse. 'Did dit dah da da la la dit dah, da da da...' She and her friend Audrey did it – one of them would send and one of them would receive. You couldn't be nervous – you had to just *get it*, quick, otherwise the Germans were going to listen in and work out where they were hiding.

So I was really into that. Running, jumping, hiding, sticking in flags. I wanted to do that because I *am* a male Emma Peel.

When I ended up stealing make-up at fifteen, my stepmother said, 'Is this all about this *Who Dares Wins* stuff?' I said, 'Sort of.' *Who Dares – Is A Transvestite*, actually. I couldn't tell her that until I came out.

I did break into Pinewood Studios when I was fifteen. I crept around Pinewood and broke into Elstree. I found out where they were on the map and I thought, someone might go creeping here, and get a job in a creeping film.

When I was sixteen, I started watching the credits on films and I thought, there's a *lot* of information here. I learned the names of the people who worked on the films. I just thought, learn it all, watch the credits. Pinewood Studios, Iver Heath. I thought, that's a *place*, Iver Heath. So I looked it up. I took a train to London, a tube to Uxbridge, a bus to Iver Heath, got out, walked down the road and came up to this gabled entrance. I said, 'Can I have a look around?' and they said, 'Fuck off.' I said, 'No, I've come, I saw it on a map, I've got to be in films.' And that was it: 'Fuck off.'

I thought, I'm not going home. There must be another way of getting in. There was another entrance, which was usually used as an exit. It's got a drawbridge thing, more of a sub-Checkpoint Charlie. I saw this guy just walk in so I thought, well, I'm fifteen, I'll walk in like I know what I'm doing, because luckily on films they have kids working on things, and I just walked in. And I was scribbling the names of editors down off doors – I had to walk round with that air of 'I know exactly why I'm here' in case someone walked past.

There was something happening on the Bond stage and I was going to look in there but I just thought, as soon as I get inside a stage door someone's going to go, 'What are *you* doin' here? Aren't you an illegal entrant person?' I thought I'd get shot so I listened through the door.

So that, and Elstree. Elstree I climbed under the wire fence and got right underneath it – my inverse of *The Great Escape* – and I was picked up by security instantly, which was completely useless. I thought they'd go, 'Creeping kid!' and put me in a film or there'd be signs – WANTED: KID TO BE IN FILMS.

I told this story to the *Avengers* producer when they were offering me the part of Bailey and he phoned ahead to the doorman at Pinewood Studios. So when we got back in the car, the doorman went, 'Welcome back to Pinewood Studios, Mr Izzard!' And that was 20 years later.

But I tended to break into whatever when I needed things. I *needed* to

see these comedy programmes, I *needed* to get hold of make-up. It wasn't frivolous – I wouldn't go and steal sausages. It was war.

So I did *The Avengers* and I went up to Edinburgh and they showed *The Man Who Would Be King* at the Edinburgh Festival and I was Sean Connery's guest. Michael Caine was there too. It was Sean Connery's birthday and they asked me, 'Could you get everyone to sing Happy Birthday to Sean Connery, because you've done this kind of stuff?' So I got up and said, 'Right, we're going to do this. It's a bit wanky but anyway, we'll get this over with,' and sang Happy Birthday into a microphone.

When I was ten, I couldn't have envisaged myself doing that, but I did try to envisage myself being in films as a henchman. Singing Happy Birthday to Sean Connery – that was on a different planet.

Sean Connery played the big game on a world stage and that's all I'm interested in, which is ambition but I don't think ambition has to be bad. If you're trying to make creative things and the whole world says, 'Hey! That's interesting!' that seems to be quite positive and groovy. If you're just trying to get a number of babies on spikes, that's the bad part. Ambition is a bad word in Britain and I think that's bullshit.

Sometimes you just have to do quite dickheady things. I went back to Eastbourne, where I used to go to school, in a big black stretch limo. Which is quite hard to do, because for some reason all the limousines in

Joe, a fun old guy, who I met on the streets of New York

England are white. I went back and I think everyone thought I was a real dickhead. Which was probably true. It was just for the fun of it.

At school, I worked quite hard until I got O-levels – I got 12, I was collecting them – and then I thought, what a boring fucker. I'm not rebellious at all. I'm not cool. I didn't really want to rebel. I was a comedy nut and a film nut more than a music nut, and fashion was more linked into music, and I wasn't really getting into punk. I couldn't work out what I wanted to rebel about. I didn't want to rebel for rebelling's sake, so in the end... when I got to A-levels I just stopped working. I thought, that'll make me cool. I'll just stop working. But then I knew nothing and A-levels came up and I had to start working again.

Part of the problem might have been dsylexia. My writing is all over the shop. When you're dyslexic, your writing is terrible. I am partially dyslexic and that's why I think laterally. I think a lot of creative people are

dyslexic. If you're dyslexic your spelling is phonetic, your writing is kind of all over the place and you jump from idea to idea.

I'm mildly dyslexic – certainly enough to have bad spelling and stuff like that. You can get teased at school horribly because your linear thinking doesn't really work. Dyslexic kids have got into my stuff – they just like it. They like my videos because mentally I jump around.

I'd like to learn to fly, although I used to throw up whenever I flew. I'd like to fly hang-gliders. *The Thomas Crowne Affair*, Steve McQueen. This is where I am. I would have been in the SAS, but then I realised they kill people with interesting bits of barbed wire. There's a murder-necessity part to being in the SAS.

I did want to be in a Jeep with the twin Vickers machine guns strapped to the bonnet in World War II. You felt like it was a good war to fight, a war to stop this shithead holding all of Europe and invading Britain. We would have fallen if we hadn't won the Battle of Britain.

I did a DJ thing on Radio One a couple of times and I got a tape of Churchill's speeches. I played a bit of it because there were two very salient points which I don't think people in Britain realise. One, if they'd invaded, we'd have been fucked. F.U.C.K.E.D. We hadn't got the guns, we hadn't been making guns, we hadn't been making tanks.

Churchill went down to Saint Margaret's Bay and there's one gun emplacement. This is a place where my parents went on their leave from Aden. I might have been conceived there. Which wouldn't have happened if the Nazis had won... but the guy who had the gun said, 'Mr Churchill, we've got five shells. Can we practise with one of them, so we know how the gun works?' And he said, 'No. Save them all for when the enemy come.' So they only had five shells. What would *that* stop?

The other thing was Churchill would come up with lines that people would grab hold of, like, 'We will fight them on the beaches.' People would go, 'Yeah, yeah, I'll go for that.' He had one line in case the Nazis invaded, which was 'You can always take one of them with you.' Which is heavy duty. Churchill was good with a one-liner.

Shitheads keep coming round. Hitler disappeared, Saddam Hussein came along, Stalin stuck around. Bosnia – bunch of shitheads. And now they've set up a world court for crimes against humanity. Everyone except America voted for it, because America are worried they're going to do covert operations somewhere and get taken to court. Apparently America are not working with the UN any more. They're saying, 'The UN slows us down. Let's go and do our own stuff.' It's what's been done throughout the entire history of human beings; if you've got the warships, just go and do it. The British did it, and the French, the Spanish, the Germans – whoever's got the gun.

I always wanted to be in the *Aliens* movie, to be the guy who was the android: 'I gotta go in and repatch the antenna to link it up and then I'll adjust it by remote in the other plane.' I love all that bullshit. Except for him climbing through the drainpipe. I couldn't do that. I get great satisfaction from mending things that aren't working. I'd love to have been an inventor. In fact, I still *want* to be an inventor.

I love *Blade Runner*. There's a good film. In the eighties I was hanging around Leicester Square, thinking, how do I start my career? They had this thing of putting televisions in cinema foyers to show the trailers. And I used to stand there watching them because I couldn't afford to see the film. I've often thought about what the future will be like, and when *Blade Runner* came out I thought, we've all got to get one of those flying cars!

I totally loved the idea of outer space. I remember getting free rockets in certain breakfast cereal packets. Certainly there was paraphernalia. Mercury and Apollo stickers. You'd get an astronaut or you'd send off for a rocket. The toys that were free were exciting but the ones you had to save a number of tokens for were annoying. I couldn't be arsed. Except for this geography project.

I won a geography project at school. I wrote it about North Sea Oil, and my dad worked for an oil company, so I got this big glossy pull-out on North Sea Oil, the Forties Field. It had one of these overlays, where you have an image with a piece of plastic on it and you pull it back and

I couldn't work out what I wanted to rebel about. I didn't want to rebel for rebelling's sake, so in the end... when I got to A-levels I just stopped working. I thought, that'll make me cool

I throw up on boats, trains, coaches, cars – trains is interesting, because who throws up on a *train*?

it forms into, in this case, a drilling rig. So I cut that out of the brochure and dumped it into my project – 'Oh, that's very nice…' I just copied a lot of stuff out of a book. And then Kellogg's Cornflakes had this offer – 'Send off to get your free oil rig with Kellogg's Cornflakes', so that was one I *did* get all the tokens for, those tabs on breakfast cereal. And I won first prize in geography.

I was really stupid, though, because the prize was a certain amount of money to spend on books, and I thought you had to spend it on books to do with geography. So I got a load of dry books on geography. Kids were going up and getting all these novels and interesting books and I got *Geography! Made More Tedious!* by Professor Dry Bastard.

So I screwed that one up, but it served me right.

But I was so pleased that the space missions happened. My mind just exploded. I wasn't really aware of the space race. For me it was just the Americans and breakfast cereal and getting little badges and broken rockets and landing on the moon and…watching it in Bishop's Stortford on television.

I felt it was pretty special, landing on the moon. But I think after a while, people just thought, what? We're only going to come back from the moon with … more *rock*? Oh… We need cheaper rocket fuel. We need to be able to travel at warp speed, even though it doesn't exist. Yet.

I was fascinated by this thing of being on the moon. I saw these educational programmes late one night. They were showing these probes flying to Mercury and Venus, which was fascinating. I love all that. I sat up at four in the morning watching these programmes going on endlessly, and I realised that they were there for teachers to tape and use the next day.

I always thought space sickness would be a problem. I have real problems with travel sickness so...space sickness? Wow! Apparently everyone gets it, even people who don't get travel sickness. So that would be a problem. I don't know what the symptoms are. Throwing up, probably.

I throw up on boats, trains, coaches, cars – trains is interesting, because who throws up on a *train*? That was through nerves really. I was airsick before we got to the airport once. Bikes ... I haven't been sick on a bike.

So I get into outer space and I'm going to be the Chuck Your Guts Up Person. And also it's more difficult because when you throw up in zero gravity, you can't put your head in the toilet, because the toilet's above your head. There's an updraft and a side draft.

I always thought I wouldn't want to go into space but now I think I would. And the take-off... I saw an episode of *Superman* and they had to cancel the shuttle take-off because there was a bomb on board and Superman pushed the shuttle up into space. And it looked quite boring because it was just this guy lifting up the thing with no exhaust. When a rocket lifts off, it needs that immense burst of energy, and all the flames shooting out, and you're just watching it and thinking, Go! Go! Fucking go! A complete emotional experience.

Once I knew there was a European Space Agency, I just wanted us to go into space and have Europeans up there. Who's going to be the first European on Mars? That's what I want to know. *I* won't be – I'll come along in the second wave. Do the gig. The ENSA of space travel.

I love *The Right Stuff*. It's a very powerful film. Sam Shepard – how cool is he? A playwright *and* an actor. I don't really know his plays because I don't read plays. But he didn't write *Run For Your Vicar*. He didn't write *Don't Put Your Knickers On Your Head Mrs Worthington*.

It's so impressive to write great plays *and* be Mr Cool. Sam Shepard played Chuck Yeager, the guy who broke Mach 1. Interestingly, the big advisor on *The Right Stuff* was Chuck Yeagar, so *that's* why Sam Shepard looked damn cool, with Yeager going 'No, I think I looked cooler than that, Sam.' When it came out, it was supposed to be this big hit – 'This one's gonna really shoot' – and it didn't quite shoot, like *Blade Runner*. But I can watch it again and again and again.

That whole time, the space race between the Americans and the Russians, was amazing. I have

Living on the moon would be fantastic. 'Let's go out and…roll around in some grey dust.' Bouncy castles would be really pointless up there

this memory of the 1963 missile crisis with the two fleets: this memory that I was listening to it on the radio. I don't know whether they *were* covering it live on the radio or not – 'And the Russians now, the Russian fleet is turning round…' I don't think they could have done, but you do get false memories you haven't seen but think you have.

There's very few books I read. When I was a kid I read *Lord of the Rings* type books and sci-fi books. *Lord of the Rings* all seemed to be about a past future, like ancient aliens. *Lord of the Rings*, *The Hobbit*, the *Narnia* series… Lewis Carroll, to an extent. I liked *Alice Through The Looking Glass* – I liked the surrealism. I liked the chessboard idea and the trains and old shops and chess pieces. I like those worlds. They're escapist.

I used to read Isaac Asimov, the famous science fiction writer, but I just don't read novels like I should. People say, 'Ooh, have you read… these people of literature, these novels by these people?' and I go, 'No.' 'Do you know this author?' 'No.' 'Have you read this play?' 'No.'

I'm very visually stimulated, even though I was very slow to have a visual sense. I had a very undeveloped sense of, 'Oh, I like the shape of that: I like that mirror at the back. Those columns don't work. Mmm, that lighting's a bit messy over there.' I've been quite blocked in that area. I'm now trying to develop that.

It is something you appreciate when you're older. Maybe it's because when you're a kid you want to get your career going and get in the action. Once you've got the action going, you want to open your eyes and sit there and go, '*Ohhwaaah*,' and smoke a pipe. I used to have problems appreciating the view, but now I *can*. Especially being in London for long

periods of time, I really appreciate the countryside now.

I still love the South Downs, especially on the north side where you can look out across southern England. It drops away in such an amazing way. It's the best angle of a hill you can have without it being a cliff and thinking, 'Bloody hell, I'm going to fall and kill myself.'

It's really quite dramatic but not dangerous. You can actually go and sit on that hill. It's 300 foot high and on a sunny day you can see for miles. You feel on top of the world. You look down on a lot of fields going out about 50 miles each way. And there's no noise up there. There's no motorway, there's no houses up there. Maybe a tractor or two, but not many crops. It's kind of wild. A lot of *The Prisoner* was shot up there. There's bomb craters up there, and there's bramble.

It's nice. It's got nothing to do with space travel, though.

They're taking bookings for the first moon trips. I was thinking, aha! A gig on the moon. It would be kind of antiseptic. But you could do all those jokes, all the crap ones. 'Hey! So... where are you from?' 'The moon.' 'Hey! Me too!' Some kid will be born there. They're going to go there and there'll be some sort of settlement there, and some kid'll be born on the moon.

Living on the moon would be fantastic in a way that you could look up and say, 'Fucking hell, the earth is my moon.' To have that in your sky must be amazing, but you'd probably be on the moon going, 'I wish I could go to the earth. The earth looks phenomenal. Let's go out and... ..roll around in some grey dust.' I suppose bouncy castles would be really pointless up there.

Yeah, I'd go there. I'd do a gig on the moon.

SEX, CRIME & SPACE

God and Stuff

New York, in a dressing room. Eddie Izzard is being interviewed. 'I tell you what my comedy is,' he confides to an eager journalist. 'It's pop culture stand-up. It's all television. All the stuff I talk about, history, whatever, it's from the History Channel, the Discovery Channel. It's all from television.'

I take very stupid things and build them to a hugely important size. I give them a lot of weight and analyse them. And I also take large subjects and talk crap about them. I talk about Hannibal attacking the Romans with elephants and then getting into elephant-skiing, because they were going to use skis, of course, but there weren't any – 'Fresh out of skis. Lots of elephants!' 'Are they good at skiing?' 'Yeah, not bad. Try 'em out. What size are you?' And then you go on and on and on, giving more and more details about something that's obviously bullshit. It is better if the idea can resonate and see if it feels like it works.

I do like taking trivial things and just extrapolating them. Jesus in flip-flops was one. It's all about how Jesus must have worn flip-flops because it's a hot country where people always wear flip-flops. You never hear, 'Jesus and his disciples tore down the road in their flip-flops,' because you have to curl your toes over to run, as you will know if you've ever run for the bus in flip-flops. You have to curl your toes over otherwise they come off.

That's why the Romans were the master race because they had flip-flops with extra tie-ups that went all the way up the leg. So I just went on and on about Jesus in flip-flops and how they didn't have stuff in the Bible saying, 'Look out, it's the rozzers! Run! It's the fuzz, get out of here!'

I went on about Matthew, Mark, Luke and John. Religion comes up a lot. That's for twelve years of going to these schools that had adults with droning voices going, 'And the sermon is this, and we shall now sing hymn number 405…' It was so dreary and it *wasn't my choice of faith*.

[Jesus to Joseph]: 'My dad, a carpenter? He's a supply carpenter! Look at that angle, it's all over the shop. Look at that door frame. Dad, look, the handle's come off!'

I even got confirmed. You had to go to a church thing on Sunday and there was an evening service, which was three-quarters of an hour, and a morning one at eight o'clock which was half-an-hour, if you were confirmed. So I thought, let's get confirmed, then I can save a quarter of an hour. So I had this whole ceremony I had to go through to get confirmed, just so I could cut out fifteen minutes off the service. You get something to eat, early in the morning, and some wine.

I did get sort of semi-religious at one point. I was about twelve and I'd read a lot of those religion-made-easy, Christianity-here-it-is stuff. I still think that he was interesting, Jesus. I think he existed. I like conversations between him and God, God calling him Jeezy Creezy. 'Dad, don't call me Jeezy Creezy!' 'All right. Look, Jeezy Creezy…' 'Jesus Christ!'

That's what my dad used to say to me a lot. 'Jesus Christ, boy!'

There's no sense of humour. Religions have no sense of humour and they never update. *Those* are the two things which screw religion. I don't know the religions in-depth, but all of them seem to have similar ideals. It's not as simple as, 'Oh, one's about hacking limbs off and one's about…' You tend to think that Islam's all beheading and chopping hands off, but there's probably a lot of 'do unto others as you would like them to do unto you' stuff there as well.

But religions are constantly outdated. They have to keep pace with society as that's what *we* have to do. We have to do it with our morals and with our laws – secular societies are always updating.

And a sense of humour is needed, otherwise everyone becomes very po-faced. I'm sure Jesus used to have a laugh, go round his dad's house: 'Look at this! It doesn't work! My dad, a carpenter? He's a supply carpenter! Look at that angle, it's all over the shop. Look at that door frame. Dad,

look, the handle's come off!' 'Come on, Jesus, don't go on about me.' 'I'm not your son, Dad.' 'Don't rub it in, son!'

It's the height of blasphemy, but if an ordinary woman came home and said, 'Someone's had sex with me and they had wings and I'm having a baby,' then that would just seem like a far-fetched story. But there's no humour in religion and there's very little flexibility because the ideas were written down long ago and there is a strong resistance to them being updated.

I had this routine that Jesus said, 'Hey.. sew some seeds, you grow good crops. If you put it on good land, good crops. If you put it on stony ground, it doesn't work. Bit of an analogy there, OK? Get the swing of it?'

But Jesus wasn't going around saying, 'The meek shall inherit the earth ... ooh, that's good, write that down. Peter, get that down. That could be in your gospel.' And Mark's going, 'What about *my* gospel?' 'All right, I'll do one for you. The socks of the world must be washed often.' 'That's not as good as Peter's!' 'All right, I'll do you another one.' It was 100 years later before they started writing these gospels. And why do the apostles have English names?

I suppose a lot of people who are religious don't question their religion. All this middle-class, 'Hello, vicar, tombola, weekend, pin-the-tail-on-the-sponge-cake...' And now there's the Vatican Bank, and all that money-laundering, and the Mafia. It just comes back to where it all started from. Jesus over-turned all the tables in the temple ... and now they have the Vatican Bank. But I suppose they've got to have money in *some* shape or form. They've got to buy things. Unless they give all their money to a bloke called Fred.

You used to be able to donate money and you'd go to heaven.

Malcolm McLaren went to court over *Never Mind The Bollocks...Here's The Sex Pistols,* because 'bollocks' was supposed to be a dirty word and so they weren't allowing it in the shops, or something like that. But in court they proved it was historically a word that was used in the Middle Ages, when people were going round being very religious and 'Give me your money and then you will get to heaven!' and 'The Lord said this' and they were making shit up and just talking bollocks.

And it was *called* 'talking bollocks'. It's great that it harkens back to there. And no-one in America knows what it means. I had someone on

Now there's the Vatican Bank, and all that money-laundering, and the Mafia. Jesus over-turned all the tables in the temple... and now they have the Vatican Bank

radio in the US saying to me, 'So, bollocks – can you talk about bollocks?'

My parents weren't religious really. My dad's religion is 'as long as you're happy.' Fifties hippy. It makes sense to me. It's quite simple, but it's what humans are all about – trying to be happy.

The Buddhism religion interests me, the middle way, because I am a radical liberal. The extremist parties have got some interesting points of course. Like 'if everyone fucking agrees with me, God damn, we could get some stuff shifted as long as we shoot these buggers over here who disagree.' But then you become a psychotic maniac. The sign of maturity

is being able to see the other person's point of view. It's having doubt and saying, 'I see your point.' Being open-minded. But doubt also scares the shit out of people.

I'm interested in this idea of weighing things up, getting a balance, and particularly in the situation in Northern Ireland, because I used to live there. If you say compromise, the hardline Protestants say, 'No.' If you say balance, they say, 'No.' These are the hardliners. I think 98% of people are saying, 'Let's get on with it, it's not worth it. What are we carving up here?' But the people who are very stubborn are just going, 'No, no, no, no...' That's what the Orange Order seems to be all about, always saying no. And they've found that by continually saying no, eventually they've made people give in. Compromise is seen as surrender.

Buddhism has the idea of the middle way. I don't know much about Buddhism – but I did see that film with Keanu Reeves in, so that's research for you. I don't know why Buddha was so *big* – probably all that meditation and no exercise puts the pounds on – but I do like this idea of the middle way, the balanced route. But if you're in the middle, people do say, 'Ah, you're wishy-washy, you don't know what to think.' That's why you have to be radical about it. A radically wishy-washy person.

The year 2000 will be a big anti-climax. Can anyone remember anything interesting happening in 1900? Or 1800? It's just another year

I think the year 2000 will be a big anti-climax. Nothing interesting will happen. There'll be a big build-up to it but... can anyone remember anything interesting happening in 1900? Or 1800? It's just another year. We expect things to happen, but they won't.

When I think of all the chemical weapons that are in the world, I do feel, 'Surely some fucker's going to get hold of something and use it!' You hear about how a small amount of chemical weapons can create so much devastation. I think they did some scenarios in America and realised that no-one's ready for a chemical terrorist attack.

It seems surprising that it hasn't happened already. And there isn't going to be a leaflet – 'Coping With Chemical Terrorist Attacks In Your Street'. I can't really see how that's going to work. 'If you are attacked with chemical weapons – hide in a cupboard forever and breathe through a tea bag.'

My two theories of outer space: one is that we're the only people and there's no-one else there in the rest of space and it's really scary. Or version two, which is also really scary: there's lots of people out there and we don't know what they're going to be like. So on the one hand, kind of scary and on the other hand... kind of scary. The-balanced but scary-view.

I think space is circular. I was reading some Native American philosophy, one of these small books of Native American wisdom, and they said everything moves in a circular pattern. You move like a child when you're young and return to move like a child when you're old. A circular thing. I have a theory of space (I have a lot of them). People say, 'Where's the edge of space?' There isn't one – space is circular. It's kind of a vast idea, so we can't quite comprehend it.

Like up in space you can stand any which way up because there's no gravity – how could you understand that back in the 1600s? So the earth is flat – and it looks flat when you look at it, but in fact if you start in one place and go on for a long time you come back to the same place. I think everything is curves. All the planets are curves, all the trajectories around the sun, they're all curved. Curves, curves, curves, fucking everywhere. Therefore God must be curvy! God must be a woman!

If you stand in space and go anywhere for infinity years, you come back to the same place. The end of the universe is where you started from. Where's the end of the earth? You're always in the middle of it. It's the only thing that makes any sense, that space is curved and wherever you are, you're in the middle. Circles seem to be somewhere in there. Stephen Hawking's got this string theory. How does that go? I don't know! That's what I *need* to know. I must read a book.

But everything is simple as well. There was this *Horizon* special about the discovery of DNA with Jeff Goldblum, and the big thing in it was they didn't know what DNA looked like, but he said, 'It's got to be pretty.' They didn't know what DNA looked like or where it was, but, 'It's got to be pretty. Truth is pretty.'

Circles. Being hyper-trendy and looking like a dickhead is a circle, except it joins up at the back. You have to look like a dickhead to be hyper-trendy. But it only goes one way round. You can't actually look like a dickhead and say, 'Look, I'm hip.' Hip people would say, 'Look, we've been moving from looking just kind of trendy up to hip here, and *you* can't just arrive and say, "I'm hip," just 'cos you look like a dickhead.'

Political circles, like the anarchists – are they extreme left wing or are they akin to the libertarians, who are sort of right wing anarchists? The extreme communists and the Nazis, who become totalitarian. This weird circle thing that goes through everything. It's also a balancing thing. People are obsessed with looking back as well as looking forward.

I'm interested in important subjects and interested in crap. And sometimes the important subjects seem to get terribly weighty and boring and I've just been waffling on about them, so I just talk crap about them. And the small ideas just give them this big context, this big backdrop.

If you stand in space and go anywhere for infinity years, you come back to the same place. The end of the universe is where you started from

And that's almost like the Tarantino balance of excessive violence and inane gossip. Balance. For me, wearing make-up and being ballsy, that's what I've got to do. If I was all effete all the time, just going, 'Wuh wobble wuh,' it wouldn't work.

I don't think there's a divine plan behind the layout of the universe. I'd go for a mixture. I'd go for a certain karma thing that happens on this world, and therefore I think it could happen everywhere. I do believe that what goes around comes around. Maybe that's just ice cream vans.

I think there's a Mother Nature thing – procreation is necessary and therefore it happens – but I don't believe in a big old bearded guy up there going, 'And now – chestnut trees! I'll make Sparta today...' So I go for the random thing, but within certain universal laws.

I think there must be other people out there. It makes sense. I mean the idea that *we're* the only planet... it does look like we exist by luck, but we're fantastically sophisticated. You only have to look around a restaurant. Everything from the paintings on the wall to the design. Whether the chairs go with the tables, the clothes people are wearing, mobile phones.

Take the body. All these bits in the brain and we only use a third of it. Then we get on computers and we only use a third of those. We never use the full capacity. You have a car and you drive along at 30 or 40 miles an hour but you don't go flat out. You don't want to drive at 200 miles an hour all the time.

It's all connected to your capacity for dealing with danger or something like that. Like when you get attacked, maybe that's when all of your brain kicks in and works.

So in conclusion, I've just re-read everything that I've said here and I really do talk a lot of crap. Some of it is pithy and wry and a deal of it seems to come from Captain Pompous and His Inflatable Ego. I've noticed that words are much more powerful when written down instead of just spoken. This may seem bloody obvious but I don't write my stand-up – I just talk it.

So if you do come across a passage that you think is bollocks, just take it out and wear it as a hat.